CLINGING TO THE ICEBERG

Writing for a living on the stage and in Hollywood

Ron Hutchinson

CLINGING TO THE ICEBERG

WRITING FOR A LIVING ON THE STAGE AND IN HOLLYWOOD

OBERON BOOKS
LONDON

WWW.OBERONBOOKS.COM

First published in 2017 by Oberon Books Ltd
521 Caledonian Road, London N7 9RH
Tel: +44 (0) 20 7607 3637 / Fax: +44 (0) 20 7607 3629
e-mail: info@oberonbooks.com
www.oberonbooks.com

A catalogue record for this book is available from the British Library.

PB ISBN: 978-1-78682-220-8
E ISBN: 978-1-78682-221-5

Printed and bound by 4EDGE Limited, Hockley, Essex, UK.
eBook conversion by CPI Group (UK) Ltd, Croydon, CR0 4YY.

FOR ALISA

PREFACE

Ron Hutchinson is a funny man. I don't mean weird funny, although he is a little weird, I mean Funny! Laugh out loud funny, slap the table funny, summon your wife into the room and say, "Read this! The hell with the bacon, Read This Right Now" funny. He has written a book, *Clinging To The Iceberg*, or is it two books, one about his life and his work, and and the other, an instruction manual, of sorts, *How To Write For And Sell To Hollywood*, and they are both falling-down funny. And smart, strong, unflinching analyses of the movie and television industries, and their desperate and eternal need for Material! Writing! Good writing, bad writing, junk, genius, ridiculous day-time soap opera shit, or powerful, and important, art-house or prime-time pieces of, dare I say it, Art? Mr. Hutchinson knows both of these categories well. But Ron is a good writer. He is, in fact, a great writer. A serious, prize-winning writer. He has written several important plays, two of which I was privileged to be a part of, all of which were gratefully received by audiences and critics alike. Inevitably, Ron's uproarious, powerful and dark creations were discovered by Hollywood, and he was bundled off to La La land, to money, and the Palm restaurant, and chauffered Town Cars, and money, and tailored Italian suits (I swear, I met him for dinner once, and he was wearing one, he looked great, too) and did I mention the money? Ron discovered, or was discovered by, the exotic, mink-lined sweatshop called Re-write Land, and he was a natural for it. Ron possesses a powerful, searching curiosity, and he loves to study and analyze, and then write about whatever subject the ailing script explores. In a week, or two, he invariably knows as much about the subject as the credited writer, or more, and his fixes make the material whole again, and usually better. And the money is great. Ridiculous, in fact, but when you consider that a substantial amount of money has already bled out on the project, a tightly-written, imaginative tourniquet, conceived and applied by Doctor Hutchinson, makes perfect sense. Hollywood sense, which should not be confused with sensible sense. Anyway, these two books, or one book with multiple personalities must be read. They are drop dead funny, and smart as hell, and important, if you really want to be a writer, and really important if you just want to have a good time. Let me finish with a couple of good quotes from the man himself. Hors d'oevres, so to speak, not to spoil the banquet Mr. Hutchinson has provided, but to stimulate your appetite for more.

"True creativity lies on the borderline between chaos and discipline. Too much chaos and the thing will never cohere. Too much discipline and the juice is squeezed out of it."

"Don't write about what you know. Write about who you are. The first is journalism. The second, art. And that's the fish we're frying."

Brian Dennehy, 2017

INTRODUCTION

Most of what you think you know about how movies and television get made is wrong. Pretty much all the advice you'll find in screenwriting manuals is useless except as a tool for analyzing other people's scripts. The majority of those who've authored those texts have had few or zero projects produced.

Even those that have ignore the central role the subconscious has in the daily life of a working writer. They can't tell you of the craziness of the production process because they've never been involved in it. They can't tell you of the inner journey of the writer's life because they've never walked it.

Don't get me wrong. They have their uses, if what you're looking for is a way to talk about the movies you've just seen. As a practical guide to writing your own script, not so much. It's the difference between sitting in the bleachers analyzing the play and being on the field.

Statistics show that most exercise equipment is used once and left in the attic to gather dust. I'd guess that's the fate of most How To screenwriting books, with their bullet points, lists and numbered rules. There are a few of those here but they're signposts to performing the act of writing, not deconstructing that of others.

When I taught at the American Film Institute I sent students who used any phrase taken from a screenwriting manual out of the room for five minutes. When the pieces of the script they'd taken apart were lying on the garage floor, they were still no nearer to creating their own original work.

What the manuals lack in addition to practical help is passion. That comes from the gut and the heart and the subconscious. To write anything of meaning that has your own mark on it you need to harness those in the service of your passion. This book can help you do that. If it doesn't, toss it into the attic along with the stationary rowing equipment and Six Pack Abs in Five Minutes a Day machine.

*

I've won an Emmy, had several Emmy nominations and won many other awards for writing for the screen and the stage; had over two hundred hours of drama and comedy produced internationally; made a good living in Hollywood and even managed to make several million dollars from one of my stage plays. When I taught at the AFI I was concerned that my students should aim for the only writing awards that matter, the ones with money attached.

As well as tales of Marlon Brando, David Hockney and Elizabeth Taylor you'll find Borges, Thomas Mann, Hegel and Nabokov in here, too. Plus a team of academic economists whose work also offers surprising insights into writing screenplays, coping with the demands of production and staying emotionally and mentally intact as your career progresses.

*

When I decided to go to Hollywood to work, an eminent British television producer wished me *bon voyage* with the cheering words *It won't work out for you. It never does when Brit writers go there. Nobody will care that you were Writer-In-Residence at the Royal Shakespeare*

Theatre or all the rest of it. You'll be back with your tail between your legs inside two years.

This prophecy seemed to be confirmed when my taxi driver at LAX turned out to be a morose Scot – is there any other kind? – who had come to LA to direct. It clearly hadn't worked out for him in what he called, as I fumbled for the fare in complete depression, a gold-lined sewer.

I was drinking in those days and my nightly refuge soon became the Molly Malone pub on Fairfax Avenue. A fixture at the bar was an ancient who attracted my attention by launching for no apparent reason a foul-mouthed tirade against *That bastard, Sean O'Casey.* He claimed to have been a promising young actor in the 1940s, lured to Hollywood to play the lead in a movie version of one of the truculent Hibernian's stage plays – I forget which.

The project had failed to launch and he'd decided to stay on, playing bit parts as the comic Irish relief until he was replaced by American actors faking Irish accents because his wasn't authentic enough for the movie audience.

Embittered, feeling the sting of a failure which he blamed on the playwright rather than the studio, he had settled on the bar stool. For life. By chance and cheek somehow I avoided this fate. At one point I had a term deal at Dreamworks, which sent me a check for sixteen thousand dollars every Wednesday for the two years of my contract; despite the fact that internal politics meant that I never actually wrote a word for them for eighteen months.

So easily did the money seem to come in that at one point I found lying on the floor four of those checks which we hadn't taken to the bank. They may still be uncashed. I'd pretty much given up writing stage plays at that point but had so much time on my hands at Dreamworks that I decided to go back to it. This determination was helped by the fact that Steven Daldry wanted to revive *Rat In The Skull,* an earlier play of mine which premiered at the Royal Court.

After the revival in the West End the bit was between my teeth again. I turned back to the theatre and used the money that Steven Spielberg, Jeffrey Katzenberg and David Geffen were paying me as a subsidy for the stage. This is the place to thank them for their generous if unwitting subvention.

Of course, sheer weight of numbers of hours produced, either on stage or the screen is not in itself guarantee of quality. When Victor Mature was refused membership of the Bel Air Country Club on the grounds that he was an actor he protested that after making over fifty movies in Hollywood no one could possibly call him that.

*

I went to The Big Avocado to learn, write and later teach the linear Hollywood narrative; the basic three act structure of the studio-made movie or television screenplay which has dominated the screens globally since motion pictures became more than a novelty in the Nickelodeons. It has its limitations and in the wrong hands is mere formula but in the right ones is an unbeatable tool for delivering narrative, character arc and exposition of theme to an international audience.

An early review of *Lady Chatterley's Lover* said that it had much good advice to offer in the management of a small game estate in the English Midlands but that, regrettably, some extraneous material had been included. Hopefully everything in these pages is to the point.

That point is a simple one – to get you to be a working writer whose main income comes from doing what you love.

CONTENTS

ONE DAMN THING
AFTER ANOTHER

The Baedeker travel guides once had a symbol which meant *Worth seeing but not worth <u>going</u> to see*. To avoid your audience wishing that symbol had been plastered over your movie's poster we have to start with story.

History can be one damn thing happening after another but a compelling story has to be something more. In our Western Humanist tradition we can spot the essentials of the majority of narratives which hold our interest – there's a distinctive milieu and some kind of love story and probably a death and a moral lesson.

Very often there's a plot twist and other elements of misdirection which may include at least one character proving not to be the person we first thought we were meeting and it's all to the good if the theme develops a metaphor and that's about it.

From behind one of the most magnificent moustaches of his day the composer Edward Elgar said that you don't write music, you pluck it out of the air. It should be the same with story. Gossip is telling a story. A joke is a story. Talking about the weather and drawing up a shopping list are stories. If you can do any of those things you already have the content of a story. Now all you have to do is shape it into a dramatic narrative. That requires you, however, to understand the basics of story-telling.

Writers think in images which add up to a story. We can't help ourselves. When I adapted Arthur Miller's unproduced screenplay *The Hook* for the stage the designer, who'd worked with Miller, remarked how, when asked a question, Miller would respond with an image or an anecdote. Here are a couple of stories from my earlier life as a fraud investigator which might illustrate those basics.

*

In my twenties I achieved what so many Irishmen across the centuries have dreamed of – being paid to hang out in bars and drink. Cultivating informants was an essential part of the process and as tongues wag loosest in bars, I was given a generous amount of money each week to lubricate them. A tip led to a surveillance of one suspect. Staking out his house in the early morning, we followed as he got into his car and started driving. And driving. And driving. With us on his tail he drove the hundred miles from the English Midlands to Liverpool, where he enjoyed a leisurely breakfast.

He then led us to Manchester, Sheffield and Leeds at a steady fifty miles an hour before heading back to where we started out, many hours previously. As he turned his car around he wound the window down and with a big grin gave us the finger. It was clear that he had spotted us and had enjoyed a leisurely motoring tour of the British Isles with us in tow to amuse himself.

EM Forster wrote that *The King died and then the Queen died* is not a story but *The King died and the Queen died of grief* is a story. Until that car window went down this had been only a series of events, one damn town and motorway service station after another. Now that series of events was undeniably a story because plot, plot reversal, expectations and their confounding, character development and narrative complication were afoot.

As indeed we were, outside Leeds in driving rain when our car overheated. In the pre-cellphone age this meant a five-mile hike to a garage.

On another case, this one involving kidnap and murder, it looked for a few, brief days that I had the key to a sensational series of killings. I also had another illustration of how story works. The police had been searching for the man the Press called The Black Panther, a shotgun-wielding robber of isolated Post Offices who had already killed three postmasters.

He had also committed what was stated to be the first kidnapping for ransom in England since Richard the Lionheart's abduction when he seized the seventeen-year-old heiress Leslie Whittle, whose body was found hung in a drainage tunnel.

A grisly series of crimes and his callous treatment of his captive made him the subject of a huge manhunt, into which I was called. My role was in connection with the money orders he stole from the Post Offices. One had been cashed locally and the overworked Criminal Investigation Division cops asked me to interview the person who cashed it.

She remembered the man and gave a description that could possibly have been the suspect, although no one had gotten a really good look at him and lived. Told that she believed he resided on a nearby rough and ready caravan park, I went from door to door until given an address.

No answer at the heavily fortified front door. The windows also seemed fortified. While I was illicitly trying to extract some of his mail from the mail slot (*A gust of wind blew it at my feet, honest, My Lord,* is how to deal with this one in court) a neighbor appeared and gave me a warning. *If he finds you on his property, son, he'll blow your head off with his shotgun.* Back at the police station interest mounted.

There were many other leads being pursued by several police agencies but this one was getting increasing attention, It looked like we had our prime suspect when I checked a number of Employment Offices. They might have had a record of where he'd worked the past few years. Up came an occupation – Tunneler. Further checks showed that he had actually been on the crew which excavated the tunnels the body was found in.

Game set and match? An arrest a hundred miles away showed that every single thing which had which pointed to our guy was co-incidence. He was a bad lot and mixed up in something but he certainly wasn't The Black Panther. A cautionary tale, given the possibilities of a wrongful arrest.

In Forster's terms you could say *The King died and the Queen died of grief and then they discovered that the King wasn't dead after all.* These are the simple building blocks from which even the most immense and complicated edifices of narrative are made.

As for the part coincidence plays, it has to be handled carefully but as the Chinese say *méiyǒu qiǎohé méiyǒu gùshì* – without coincidence there is no story.

*

When I taught at the American Film Institute I was concerned that my students should know that this was about writing their own movies and not sitting in Starbucks taking other people's movies apart. This got us somewhere but there was still a long way to go.

Although these were graduate students they had little experience of real life on which to draw. What could they write about that would be fresh and new and not a re-tread of the latest movie that had just made millions of dollars? Where could they get the stories from that were going to be their bread and butter as professional writers?

The breakthrough came when one student expressed a desire to write a black comedy set in a morgue. Problem was the script was a series of smart-aleck gags that were mostly banter, the dry rot of dialogue. I told him to take a few days away from academe and arranged for him to go to the morgue of the City Coroner of Los Angeles.

This met with some resistance because it meant exposing him to the real deal, in which he might actually have to see some dead bodies. I assured him this wasn't the worst thing in the world – one of my most fascinating research trips was to a pathologist's lab where I watched five autopsies take place.

There I learned that once they open you up and take out the working bits – guts, brain, lungs – they need to stuff the cavities so the corpse looks its best for the grieving relatives. They do this – or they did at my visit – using rolled up newspapers. Not an image you could invent or relish; facing eternity with your skull and belly filled with ads for used cars and mattress sales.

My student eventually gave in and came back glowing. Not only had he seen his first corpse – an existential rite of passage – but he had learned that (a) the LA morgue had a gift shop where you could buy souvenir mugs, key chains, T-shirts and – somewhat insensitively – fridge magnets and (b) if you had sex with a corpse in California you had broken no laws.

The former could be put down to the entrepreneurial spirit of the New World. The latter to the fact that there was no force involved in screwing a stiff so it was not rape or indecent assault. True, it could be inferred that no consent had been given but neither could it be established that it had been withheld, or protest made. Needless to say, he had his movie.

Encouraged by that, I sent all my students on field trips to places such as a Marine Corps base and a school for the blind and arranged for them to work, for example, for a week in the laundry room of a four-star hotel.

I didn't ask them to come back with fully shaped narratives. A character, a detail, an insight, even a single line would be enough to pluck something from the air as Elgar plucked a note which would then lead to a phrase, a bar, a page of music and then a symphony.

*

A word of caution here. I'm all in favor of research but

A SCREENWRITER'S RESEARCH SHOULD BE A SMASH-AND-GRAB RAID ON THE SUBJECT MATTER

and not an early draft of a Ph.D. dissertation. If you have a questing mind it's too easy to get lost in the thickets of a subject, piling up the research and forgetting that one day you have to sit down and commence the screenplay. Or maybe that's the point.

A writer friend of mine wanted my opinion on a spec script he was thinking of writing. I'm not in favor of this kind of free speech but agreed to help. First off he told me the names of his characters. They were all either anagrams of the other characters' names or contained coded references to characters in other movies.

Showing me a chart, he explained the way all the names cross-referenced with each other. It was smart, witty, the product of hours of work and nothing whatsoever to do with beginning the screenplay. That wasn't even in his desk-planner yet. He still had the names of a couple of the minor characters to work out.

I don't think he ever wrote the first line. Something was holding him back and it wasn't laziness or lack of application. We're going to be talking about the subconscious and its role in a writer's life in a page or so. Is it too much of a stretch to suggest that his subconscious knew whatever strengths and intelligence he had weren't a perfect match for the business of writing commercial screenplays? As opposed to the gift that he did have, for clever word play?

I forget in which professional context the phrase *You have to do the boring stuff well* was first used. Either sports or bomb disposal, maybe. There's a heck of a lot of boring stuff involved in putting one word after another for hours at a time. Much more fun is interviewing experts on a subject or devising acrostics.

As soon as a dramatic shape suggests it, dump the research project. You can always come back to it later if there are gaps in your knowledge which are getting in the way of story or character development. Mozart said that he got the entire concerto in his head in one moment. All he had to do after that was write the notes down in the right order. That does mean, however, writing that first, vital note from which everything else flows.

LOCATION, LOCATION, LOCATION

S ome writers love being on location. Others loathe it. With luck you'll have the chance to find out what camp you're in. You'll make a sale or get flown to the set for a production polish. When that happens remember that screenwriters are not film makers and should never start to believe they are.

A film maker is someone with a baseball cap on backwards who stands in a muddy field at five in the morning demanding to know where the generators are. Their time is mostly spent arguing with the lead actress about her hair and trying to set up the next project while giving the minimum of attention to the one they're actually shooting.

The film maker's job is to pay back the bullying they're receiving from the studio by taking it out on the writer, actors, wardrobe, hair and make-up and their personal assistant and also to have an affair with one of the actors.

The writer's job is to deliver the lines to be spoken and then stay out of the way having been flown at the last minute to a rain forest in Mexico, the sand dunes of the Kalahari Desert in Namibia, the other side of the Atlas Mountains in Morocco, to the hinterlands of Inner Mongolia and China or a small town near the Great Barrier Reef in Australia.

Or Paris, Budapest, Warsaw, Lodz, Berlin, Brussels, Rome, Istanbul, Oslo, Moscow, Vienna, Dublin, Belfast, Vancouver or

Montreal – all places where I've been posted in the service of my craft.

Incoherent with jet lag you'll be met by the studio car and rushed to the set where the loss of a location or actor has meant emergency heart surgery is needed on the next day's script pages.

It's possible your only knowledge of the existing script was a quick read on the way across and maybe a look at the dailies in First Class – the Writer's Guild deal says you have to be flown top dollar anywhere over two and a half hours away from Los Angeles – and you're a little fuzzy on details. Such as who the characters are and what it's about, remembering of course that what a movie is about isn't the same as what happens in it. No matter. Like a good soldier fed into the trenches by a crazed general, your job is to put things right. *Now.*

*

Even if you do that, by the way, there's no guarantee you'll get any credit on the screen. Some years ago the Writers Guild made what some writers still see as a devil's bargain. Its members took over the task of deciding screenplay credit.

Until then things had been a bit haphazard, with all the dangers that implied of, say, the hatcheck girl the producer had just met being awarded it. This matters not just as a sop to vanity but because the on-screen credit determines how the financial pie is divided.

You might think the fairest thing to do would be to split it between everybody who has a hand in the writing process. I was the sixth and eighth writer on one movie and many movies are the product of even more hands. The Guild decided to restrict credit to a maximum of four and preferably three writers, which has the benefit of keeping things simple. In theory. In practice rules for awarding credit take up many pages of legalese which include several paragraphs on the permitted use of the ampersand.

It's an arcane process and I have done many arbitrations as a Writer's Guild member. What matters is how closely the final screenplay reflects the produced movie. This doesn't mean that the last writer on board gets credit, unless she or he substantially shapes the final product.

Confusingly to the outsider it also means that you don't get screen credit even if you were the very first writer. It's possible that the project changed so much that not even the original script's own mother would recognize it. Or want to.

*

The physical discomforts of the location can't be allowed to get in the way and often they're extreme. Generations of movie makers know the Moroccan town of Ouarzazate only too well. There's a movie studio in the desert there where much of *Lawrence of Arabia* was shot. It was also the location of the punishment battalion of the French Foreign Legion. Just outside the town, where the blacktop runs into the Sahara, is a famous road sign with a camel on it reading TIMBUKTU – 54 DAYS. You get the idea?

Now add a disused motel which is serving as the production office in which you have to write and write against the clock at that. The motel is disused because the drains do not work. It is one hundred and twenty degrees in the shade, should you find any, and every time a door opens you smell the drains.

In the next office the casting director is interviewing people of restricted growth with apparently total hearing loss as extras in the biblical epic you are engaged on and just outside the armorers are hammering metal to make swords, helmets and spear points, with extraordinary vigor.

Or imagine yourself in Swakopmund, which you will instantly recognize as the second city of Namibia; a country so remote that not even the people who live there know where it is. The tourist guides note that it's famous mainly for the dense, choking, freezing fog which envelops it for six months of every year, situated as it is between the Benguela Current and the Kalahari.

It also, thanks to its past as a German colony, has several souvenir shops with an interesting line in SS and Gestapo memorabilia. We are here because just outside it are the biggest sand dunes in the world in which the movie is being shot. I'm hard at work on revisions when my line producer decides to drink from the tap.

I'll write that again. My line producer drinks from the tap. In Swakopmund. In Namibia. Within minutes his face is as green as a leprechaun's underpants and he looks about to die. I take time off from the script to dose him with Cipro, which medication should always be part of your kit when traveling.

It cures anthrax, which gives you some idea of how powerful it is. (It does have an unfortunate side effect, however, in that if you attempt to lift heavy weights while taking it you can rupture your testicles.) Within a couple of hours of taking the tablets, he's as good as new and shouting into the phone with his previous brio. I return to my task of revising the scene which they are shooting the very next day and whose sides the actors are waiting for.

Or let's say you have been flown halfway around the world to Australia where you are to rewrite a movie starring Marlon Brando, which is set fair to be one of the legendary movie disasters of all time. It's the rainy season. The cast and crew have been here for eight weeks and the atmosphere is poisonous. There's hardly any film in the can.

That's the situation I found when I arrived and on the first night managed to cut my wrist on a piece of broken glass in my hotel room. It was quickly patched up but the very next day rumors swept the company that the new writer had taken one look at what he was up against and had tried to kill himself.

The events that ensued in what we all came to regard as our Outback Purgatory were so baroquely, blackly comic that I've turned them into a piece for the theatre. It's included at no extra charge at the rear of this volume.

*

How do you find it in yourself to keep your concentration in all this mayhem, paranoia and insanity?

There are many often competing issues to be resolved –

> THE DIRECTOR'S NEED TO MAKE THE SCENE AS BIG AS POSSIBLE VERSUS THE LINE PRODUCER'S BUDGET WORRIES.

> THE NOTES FROM THE STUDIO IN LA THAT CAME IN OVERNIGHT THAT DISAGREE WITH BOTH OF THEM.

> THE BALANCE EACH SCENE HAS TO STRIKE AGAINST ALL THE OTHER SCENES WHICH MOSTLY EXIST IN ONE PERSON'S HEAD AT THIS MOMENT – YOURS.

> THE KNOWLEDGE GLEANED FROM THE DAILIES THAT ONE ACTOR PLAYING A CHARACTER IN THAT UPCOMING SCENE ISN'T GOOD ENOUGH AND THEIR PART IS LIKELY GOING TO HAVE TO BE CUT AND THE INSISTENCE OF THE LEAD ACTOR ON THEIR VISION OF WHO THEY'RE PLAYING AND THREAT TO WALK IF IT'S NOT DONE HIS OR HER WAY.

Another factor is that you, the writer, are human too and not a dialogue machine. You've had intestinal problems of your own since learning that the burger you had last night was ostrich meat; you haven't had much sleep because the armed guards outside the hotel play cards and crack nuts very loudly all night underneath your window; you are in the middle of trying to resolve a domestic issue with your loved one many thousands of miles away and your agent is demanding you come home right away because the studio seems to be reneging on the terms of the deal that sent you there.

Having taken the gig you need to find a way to shut out the craziness all around you, refuse to be infected with the contagion of the others' panic and open yourself to what the movie is trying to say; reconnect with the grain of the screenplay which is the blueprint for it.

The autobiography of the prolific Victorian novelist Anthony Trollope has some sage, practical advice on writing under pressure. Such as

Absolutely never write for more than three hours at a stretch on any one project.

Tony T should be listened to because his acres of pages were written while he was traveling the world setting up the British post office system. He could write in a stage coach, on a sailing ship, on a train – in the gondola of a balloon, if need be.

No laptop, either. Or one of those bendy things with a light on the end that you clip to the page. Only pen, paper and candle and his own imagination and his own powers of observation and memory.

He even managed to find time to do his three hours a day – and it has to be three hours *every* day, not when you feel like it – as he toured the battlefields of the American Civil War.

There, among other things, his sharp writer's eye noted that after the battle of Gettysburg the cost of false teeth fell precipitously in Europe and the US. This was because at that time dentures were mostly made from real teeth and the best of those teeth were clearly those of young, healthy men. Young healthy men such as those mowed down in their thousands in the first war of the industrial era.

After the battles – and sometimes while they were still raging – collectors scoured the field with pliers, removing the teeth. A bonus would be finding a gold filling but any molar would do. Packed into barrels, they were shipped to Liverpool and thence to Hamburg where the gob craftsmen were based.

An index of how desperate the body count was in this new form of warfare was the one third drop in the wholesale price of dead men's teeth following on from that seminal struggle. One which only happened at Gettysburg because it had a boot factory and the Confederate Army was short of footwear.

*

I'm indebted for this information to a fascinating volume entitled *The Strange Story of False Teeth* by John Woodforde, published by Routledge & Kegan Paul which should be on the shelf of anyone interested in poking around in odd corners of history.

Trollope noted the detail but never used it. Hard to see how it could have fitted in with his gentle satires of aristocratic and clerical life but your writer's eye, like his, must always be revolving in your head, like the lamp of the Eddystone lighthouse. Whip out the notebook you will carry from now on, or tip-tap it into the Notes screen on your damned phone and one day it may come to be of use.

If Anthony Trollope could find that quiet, steady place to write from in the middle of the press of affairs, tempest, strife and stomach distress, so can you, wherever in the world your writing life will take you.

*

It's reasonable to ask why any movie would get itself into another fine mess like this. Who signed off on the screenplay and why haven't they been fired? The answer is that the script is very often the pimple on the backside of the production in the run-up to rolling the cameras.

The producers have many other things to juggle — casting, locking down locations and crew, internal studio politics and financial issues. A change in tax policy or shifting of a few percentage points in an exchange rate can torpedo the whole thing at the last minute.

Many of those crises are immediate and need to be fixed by close of the business day, whereas the finalized script isn't absolutely required until the director shouts *Action!*

That means leaving it to the last minute. The problem with leaving something to the last minute, according to C. Northcote Parkinson, is that it only gives you a minute to fix things. Movie makers seem to thrive on the pressure that puts them under. As you check into your hotel room hundreds or thousands of miles from home, you can't let that pressure get to you.

The fate of the project depends on the work you're going to do in the minutes and hours ahead, whatever else is going on around you. That's a huge responsibility and why I was happy to be known as The Rewrite Guy and proud to call myself a writer for hire.

So total had my concentration to be on the job in hand that I checked into one hotel and set to work without noticing that the room had no windows. I only realized that when my wife pointed it out when she arrived five or six days later.

Remember on your own travels to insist on a room with a window and that a month's supply of Ciprofloxacin(1-cyclopropyl-6-fluoro-4-oxo-7-(piperazin-1-yl)-quinoline-3-carboxylic acid) should always be in your luggage. Don't take my word for it. It's on the World Health Organization's list of essential medicines.

Unless you're a male weight lifter.

*

No matter how exotic the location or involving the work, at some point you have to let go of it. EM Forster – who was the least likely person in literary history to die in Coventry – compared the moment when a novel is finished to how the piano must feel when everything else in the house has been cleared out.

The great-grand-daddy of sighs of relief was probably that of Edward Gibbon after fifteen years' labor on the one and a half million words of *Decline and Fall of the Roman Empire*.

He wrote

> *After laying down my pen I took several turns in a berceau, or covered walk of acacias, which commands a prospect of the country, the lake, and the mountains. The air was temperate, the sky was serene, the silver orb of the moon was reflected from the waters, and all nature was silent.*

Okay, yes, perhaps that's too grandiose a reflection when you've just written THE END on a teen comedy zombie apocalypse movie but it's important to find a way to mark the completion of every piece of work.

In the early part of my career I went on three-day black-out drinking sprees. Latterly, no longer a drinker, I'll buy a book or go to a movie in the middle of a working day. It may seem trivial but it's a way of marking the laying aside of something which has preoccupied you for days or weeks or months. It's also saying thanks to the subconscious which has been such a crucial part of the work you've done.

*

Given the realities of screenwriting it's likely the draft you just handed in, no matter how good, may lead to being asked for another draft. Or learning that another writer has replaced you.

You can't take it personally. Writing in this medium is a series of abstentions, abandonments and partings of ways. You hand the script to your producer, your producer hands it to the director, the director hands it to the actor who then hands it to the audience. When you see what those successive hands have done to it, you may not see much, if any, of your own work in it.

Take comfort in (a) the check that you have long since cashed and (b) the character of Charles Strickland in Somerset Maughan's *The Moon And Sixpence*.

In a story loosely based on Paul Gaughan's exile in the South Seas, the painter Strickland acknowledges that, having worked night and day on a canvas whose idea has possessed him for weeks or months, on completion he could toss it aside and not look at it again. It was now worth no more to him than an old cardigan, discarded and flung on a chair.

The screenwriter John Gregory Dunne noted that when you're in The Zone the subconscious and conscious mind are pulling in tandem and everything you see or touch or hear is somehow connected with what you're working on. You open a newspaper or overhear a snatch of conversation or spot something out of the corner of your eye and realize with a shiver of joy that it's connected or could be made to be connected with a character, a plot twist or a new narrative invention.

At some point that stops. You're no longer in The Zone because your creative partner, the subconscious, knows the task is done for now. Not because of weariness with the project or desire to just get the thing delivered and out of your life. Those are front brain issues and it's dealing with the important stuff at the back of the mental store, where synthesis and integration happen.

Work closely enough with your subconscious intelligence and you will know when it's disengaging from the current project. That disengagement is final and you should listen to it and act on it.

3

STORY STRUCTURE
ON DOPEY DRIVE

There really is a Dopey Drive on the Disney lot in Burbank and the caryatids which support the main office building and executive lair are giant size figures of the dwarves themselves. It's at the same time comic, imposing and unnerving, which is any sane person's response to the Disney juggernaut which is still run like a nation state dedicated to the memory of the founder.

Entering the manicured grounds after a chirpy greeting from the security guards I always feel I'm in a version of what East Germany would have been like had State Communism actually worked.

Walt was an anally compulsive neat freak in both story structure and real life. One of the things he was proudest of at the theme park in Anaheim was the system of hidden vacuum pipes which helped the 'cast members' almost instantly dispose of the garbage left by the visitors. The chain-smoking Walt himself didn't intend to disappear any time soon even after death and on my first trip to Los Angeles I lived in close proximity to his corpse.

*

I'd been given an apartment behind a house in the very posh Hancock Park – until the 1940s restrictive covenants meant that no Jews were allowed to live there – but was puzzled by the sound of geese cackling through the night.

The owner told me that Walt had left his body to a scientist who had frozen it and was keeping it in the house directly behind hers. Excitable and quarrelsome geese are a perfect alarm system and were there to alert the pioneer cyrologist to any celebrity body snatchers who might be on the prowl.

She went on to tell me that the reason the Disney studios were in a slump at that time was because a medium had been hired to convey the de-animated animator's instructions to the board.

It seemed that Walt's sure footedness and almost uncanny ability to figure what dreams the world wanted to dream were misfiring now that he was in the Great Beyond. Or maybe his vision got lost in translation. Shortly after this a boardroom putsch led to a new regime being put in place and soon Disney was a powerhouse again and its beating heart has always been the animated division.

On a tour of it one day I was struck by the pods in which the animators crashed for a few hours' sleep, unwilling to tear themselves away from the drawing board or computer screen. I was even more struck by the, literally, hundreds of drawings on the walls, sketches for individual characters and backgrounds but, more to our point, narrative.

Walking down the length of the wall would allow you to literally see the direction the story was going. You could experiment by dropping a section or beat entirely or move it somewhere else; adjusting in real time the tactics of telling that particular tale in the service of the overall strategy.

Now I have no wish whatsoever to work in animation. Even with the help of computer imagery you need two or three years to get the piece on screen; which is often longer than your marriage may have lasted. If the show doesn't work in that first crucial box office weekend who do you go to to get those years back?

In addition (or subtraction) because of the unique demands of the form the remuneration and residuals structures are different to other scripted writing so you may be taking a real financial hit working on an animated show, even though your kids may love you more for it. Those acres of drawings, however, suggested why so many classic and contemporary animated movies have watertight plots and ruthlessly efficient character development.

You could literally see the story take shape. You could put your finger on the exact frame where one element or invention took it in the wrong direction. If a sequence didn't work it could be moved to another point in the narrative and story arc or dropped altogether. Sure, most live action movies use storyboards but those are mainly for production design and cinematography reasons. On the walls of this historic building were the X-rays and ultra-sounds which brought to physical life the interior mechanism of dramatic construction.

*

Dylan Thomas said that writing a poem was like carrying a wriggling squirming thing up a flight of stairs and trying not to drop it before you got to the top. That suggests the physicality of the process. Much is done inside the skull but the hands, our chief organ of touch, are the means by which the brain gets the thought out to the world.

Anyone who labors a keyboard or a pen will spend hours each day staring at their hands. When I look at mine I see bone spurs on the knuckles of the three fingers I type with. Forty plus years of hammering first typewriter keyboards and then computer keyboards will do that to you. That's why so few writers have secondary careers as hand models.

We *punch up* a scene or *hammer it out* or *cut* a line or are called in to *polish* a script and for many of us the work is best done standing up. Hemingway was famous for his vertical approach to the act of writing. There's much to be said for being, like him, on your feet like a boxer as you write. It not only prevents spinal problems and carpal tunnel syndrome but it makes you lean into the page instead of sitting back.

The sense that you are jabbing, ducking and weaving with the thing you are creating makes it a live and vital thing instead of flat words on the flat page. Going twelve rounds upright gets the script into your body as well as your mind. When you talk about it you will feel its shape, where it flows, where it's as lumpy as a motel mattress, where the ideas in it come to life and where they endlessly circle the runway and never touch down.

The hours you are writing are not a time-out but your real job. Put your back into it. Get out of that chair and stay on your feet when you write. Fallen arches? There are orthopedic inserts for that. Born idle? You're in the wrong business. Downloading the brain matter through the hands is a physical act and should leave you pretty much shattered. As Robert Louis Stevenson ruefully noted

EASY READING IS DAMNED HARD WRITING

and as an eminent writer on food observed, the one thing all the great chefs he'd watched had in common was that they cooked with the gas full on.

*

Projecting that totally absorbing effort every single day of your life conditions your subconscious mind to work on the project. Not known for his zingers, Maxim Gorky came out with a very solid one in –

THE TRUE HERO OF THE IMAGINATIVE LIFE
IS THE SUBCONSCIOUS

He's telling us that once the writing habit is established the hidden and more powerful part of our mind goes to work. It silently integrates and synthesizes the material that we've been working on below the layer of consciousness. This isn't Hippy Dipshit New Age Fairy Dust but practical advice on using the totality of what's inside that weird lump atop our neck.

When your hours of writing on any one project are finished, hand it over to the subconscious to work on it. When you return to it after several hours of other business or sleep, nine times out of ten those nagging problems of construction or paucity of invention which have been troubling you will have been solved. In time you will come to trust and rely on that creative partner just behind that big hole in the front of your face you look at the world through.

This only works however if you work every day, conditioning your subconscious the same way you have disciplined your frontal brain. I suspect this is the root of Hemingway's dictum to always leave something unfinished every writing session. That's the clear-cut handing over of the task which jump-starts the process.

It's not just in the world of art that Maxim's maxim applies. Mathematicians, chemists and physicists understand it and rely on it, too. Otto Szilard relates how out of the blue between one footfall and the next on a quiet London street he realized that a nuclear chain reaction was possible. The result, several removes on, was the atomic bomb and often the effect of your subconscious suddenly integrating the material it's been silently working on will feel like an explosion upstairs.

*

It's a tantalizing possibility that Gorky might have worked for Disney had he stayed in the US after his visit there in 1906, during which he wrote *I feel at home, though the language of New York is not my own, and I do not understand a word of it. I never visited a place so kindling to my imagination.*

In true early-Hollywood style he was chased out of his hotel because of a sex scandal when it was found that he shared his room with an actress and not with his wife. He then went back to Russia and ultimately to his death at Stalin's hands.

What if he'd stayed on the East Coast and crossed the Hudson River to the improbable place which birthed the first American motion picture, Fort Lee in New Jersey? He'd surely have seen the power of this new medium as a tool for mass expression and agitation.

Later he would have drifted West, to Los Angeles and Hollywoodland, in whose silent films his lack of English American would not be a problem. The politicking, backstabbing, serial betrayals, blood-letting and infighting inseparable from the entertainment business would not have fazed him, given his apprentice background in revolution.

The monsters he became the intimate and tool of – Lenin and Stalin – would have met their match in a Harry Cohn or a Louis B. Mayer. In no time at all he would have been their buddy too and instead of the dacha outside Moscow been happily ensconced at a beach house in Malibu and have swapped the dream of socialist revolution for a studio deal.

No doubt at some point his path would have crossed with Walt, which might have made a considerable difference to the plot line of *Snow White*. Those dwarves certainly needed labor representation, given the hours they worked with their only health and safety gear being red and green woolen hats.

It was not to be. The Russian returned home to the Fantasia of the workers and peasant state to become the Sorcerer's Apprentice for the creator of The Gulag. Ultimately it was Walt's vision which created a permanent revolution in the world of the imagination instead of practical affairs.

That success was founded on the genius of the linear narrative which he pioneered at feature length in *Snow White*. To this day we're all still, for better or worse, on Dopey Drive.

4

ART HOUSE VERSUS MULTIPLEX

'Have you ever seen Alexandre Fin?' asked Mr. Mybug. 'I saw him in Pepin's last film "La Plume de ma Tante", in Paris last January. Very amusing stuff. They all wore glass clothes, you know, and moved in time to a metronome.'

'Oh yeah?' said Mr. Neck. 'A frog, eh? Frogs is all under five feet…I seen that film in Paris, too. It gave me a pain. Gave me a lot of new dope, though. What not to do and all that. I've met Pepin, too. The poor egg's cuckoo.'

'Then your interest in the cinema, Mr. Neck, is *entirely* commercial? I mean, you think nothing of its aesthetic possibilities?'

'I gotta responsibility. If your frog friend had to fill fifteen thousand dollars' worth of movie seats every day, he'd have to think of a better stunt than a lot of guys wearin' glass pants.'

*

The scene is from Stella Gibbons' *Cold Comfort Farm*, which is possibly the funniest book, line for line and scene for scene, ever written. Mr. Neck is on one of his annual buying trips to the UK to shop for new actors. The book was written in 1932 but if you've spent time in today's Hollywood you'll give a yelp of recognition.

It's all there. The tough guy *patois* of the producer. The ruthless dissection of a screen player's appeal. The straightforward acceptance that this isn't brain surgery, it's business. And, the cherry on top, the split between two visions of cinema that exist today in bricks and mortar as Art House versus Multiplex.

Depending on how you look at it, I had either the good fortune to fall into the studio system straight away or the dire bad luck to miss out on the independent scene. Looking back, it doesn't seem as if I made a conscious choice but make one I did and it shaped my thirty years there.

Past is prologue, what happens in the first scene determines how the movie ends so maybe I'd better sketch my life journey to the point where the deflating Scotsman picked me at the airport on my first arrival in LA.

This isn't entirely an exercise in vanity but may help the reader understand why I chose to play the role of hired gun as opposed to that of crazed loner; why I slotted so easily into being The Rewrite Guy taking on whatever they threw my way; Page One Rewrites, Production Polishes, Dialogue Touch-Ups or Tweaks.

In your own career, you'll at some point have to decide where your talent lies and where your heart is. Sure, much of its trajectory will be down to dumb luck – being in the right place at the right time or striking up a relationship with a film maker whose vision jibes with yours.

You still need to know whether you want to fill the multiplexes with a hundred-million-dollar opening weekend or if you'd rather have your name up there on the credits of a badly lit black and white movie screened out-of-competition at the Opening Night Gala at the Bratislava Film Festival.

If the former you might have to help dumb the movie down to appeal to people with an IQ smaller than their shoe size. If the latter the most you'll likely make out of it is a complimentary ticket for the opening night gala (includes weiner schitznel buffet and no-host bar.)

Your call.

*

The arc of my career begins in Ireland, which is a pretty good early career move if you want to be a writer. My mom went mildly nuts at one point, which is another. Full bore, mat chewing crazy is of course much better but you work with what you're given.

Things got even better when we moved for the sake of her mental health from dangerous Belfast to a cottage with no running water, gas, electricity or flush toilet – there was barely a roof – in Port Muck near Mullaghbuoy on the peninsula of Islandmagee, which pretty much meant living on an island.

An island famous for three things. In 1643 all the Catholics on it were murdered by being thrown off at the clifftops at the Gobbins; the trial of eight witches in 1711 and for those who know their tubers, yes – the Red Craig potato was first grown there.

You're ahead of me already. The cottage we lived in was called The Witches House and local legend, which I backed up with later research, confirms that several of the witches lived there. Three died under investigation and the five others barely survived the brutality of being exposed in the stocks at the nearest town, Carrickfergus, every three months for a year. I later wrote a movie about this.

Was there an old woman who came out from Belfast at weekends, who sat in a rocking chair in a corner of the cottage next door and told tale after tale of Irish rebellion, as seen from the Scots-Irish, Protestant side? Yes, there was.

There was also, as you'll have expected, a rowboat that served as a ferry to take us to Larne, just across the water, whose ferryman doubled as the village drunk. Now and again he mis-read the weather and was borne, passengers and all, onto the coast of Scotland, a reasonably dangerous fourteen miles away.

Would there have been prehistoric monuments on the island and ghosts and the constant sound of the sea battering the thatch? Indeed. Was there a small rocky island, Muck Island, just offshore that could be reached by a causeway, depending on the tides, on which Captain Kydd was reputed to have buried his loot? Yes.

Was this an island of women and had always been an island of women because the land was too poor to farm and the sea too dangerous to fish so all the men went away, as mine did, in his case to be a bricklayer on the mainland? Of course. Was it not until I left for England in my early teens that I saw a television set or realized there were flush toilets, libraries, movie theaters and water that miraculously came out of taps? Naturally.

*

I had the foresight even before I was born to equip myself with a collection of relatives who were always good for a yarn. My Uncle Billy, for example, who jumped ship from the Royal Navy in Long Beach in 1938 because he saw the war coming even sooner than Churchill did.

They caught up with him in 1942 and sent him to fight in the Pacific, where his ship was sunk by a Japanese submarine. Picked up by the Australians he returned to the UK. Having lost touch with his family, whose house in Belfast had been demolished by a German bomb, he took forty years before trying to contact them again. In the meantime he raised a daughter who taught unarmed combat to the Liverpool police.

He'd heard a rumor that my mother was living in Coventry, England and wrote a letter to the local paper asking for more information. While his letter was in that city's central sorting office the Irish Republican Army blew it up and in the ensuing conflagration his letter was lost.

A couple of years later he wrote again and this time was successful. My mother visited him with her sister Edie and her husband Dave, and discovered that he was working for the Gas Board. Clearly this was a man to whom the possibility of a sudden explosion added spice to life.

The visit was a great success, marred only by the fact that Uncle Dave dropped down dead the moment he and Edie got back from the reunion. My Uncle Harry never managed to reach the war. On the troopship taking him across the Atlantic he overlooked the fact that the swimming pool in which he took his morning swim had been drained overnight. Diving in, he broke his neck and was buried in a British military cemetery in Miami.

Two things stand out. The obsession the men in my family have with the United States, in Billy's case at the risk of being shot for desertion and in Harry's a permanent connection six feet under. Given their histories and those of several other family members ranging from mildly eccentric to batshit crazy, how could I believe anything other than that the Gods of Comedy were in charge of the Universe?

*

We ended up in Coventry because there no work to be had for bricklayers in Ireland and we needed to move. My dad had been to war and then absent working on the mainland and it was time to try to live as a family.

On his way back from the war he had passed through Algiers and Palermo and Cagliari and Rome and Naples but decided of all those places to return to with us it had to be England's industrial midlands. This meant swapping green fields and the salt spray of the Irish Sea for lodgings in the sulfurous lee of a chemical plant;

lodgings hard to come by because in those days you really did see signs that said NO DOGS, BLACKS OR IRISH.

I think maybe with hindsight he saw Erin's never-ending Troubles coming again and wanted no part of them for us. Violence was always in the air in Ireland; the clearest stream would suddenly turn opaque, the stillest leaf quiver on a windless day.

Not only was Islandmagee the site of that massacre, there were the remains of a burned-out house at the end of our lane. A Catholic family had tried to move in fifty years previously. They had been fire-bombed on the first night and the charred shell of the building left as a warning to others.

One of my uncles, a policeman, was shot dead on the border in 1958 while on patrol and my otherwise gentle if slightly cracked mother talked wistfully of her childhood in Belfast where the Pope was regularly burned in effigy.

There was no getting away from threat on this move to England because Coventry had, in the years I was growing up there, one of the highest per capita murder rates in Europe. The day we arrived the kid next door asked if we were Irish and when I said Yes broke my nose.

We lived on a housing estate where domestic disputes were common and often settled by people being knocked senseless. Often, for some reason, by hitting each other with coal scuttles.

It was in this hard-scrabble, no-frills place that had been bombed flat in the war by the Luftwaffe but not flat enough, to my mind, given its soulless, concrete heart that I went to comprehensive school. How to get out? How to get out?

*

The first step was dropping out at fifteen after I brought home a school report which contained Shakespeare's line *Like Leviathan, he lifts his back above the element he lives in.* My parents couldn't make head or tail of it and nor could I. To be on the safe side I got a thump on the ear and was told I'd better get off to work as soon as possible.

Not that I minded. I'd already been working a part-time job gutting fish. On my first day I'd witnessed a fight between two of my fellow gutters wielding knives and fish gaffs, both being in competition for the calloused hand of one of the belles of the gutting tank. Blood was shed. This was adult life with a vengeance. Show me more.

Now fish gutting is a fine profession for a young man or woman starting out in life but it has to be said the emphasis is pretty much on gutting fish. For several hours a day, usually starting at five in the morning, standing in cold water with your hands and feet in ice.

One joke among my fellows on the cutting block never wearied them – filling a co-worker's wellington boots with fish guts so that, bleary eyed, the victim would step into them in the morning. Another was to collect a large tub of refuse and tip it over somebody's head while they were in the toilet cubicle. On the whole a bit like being sent back to the eighth century. B.C.

*

There followed a series of dead end job disasters including somehow being put in charge of issuing plumbing supplies for the local municipality. The clerk I'd taken over the post from whispered to me as he handed over the keys to the storeroom *You have a job for life here, mate. Don't mess it up.*

Could anything be more calculated to make young blood run cold? Advancement depended on going to a local college and getting a formal qualification in the English language. This seemed a good way to improve my very tenuous career prospects but on the sign-up evening I picked up the wrong form or went through the wrong door or otherwise messed up.

The next week I walked into what I thought was going to be a return to the classroom but was confronted by a stage on which half-dressed young women were being 'warmed up'. This seemed to be a necessary condition for them to be gotten into before the study of Speech and Drama, which was the class I had accidentally committed myself to.

It was in that class that I stepped onto a stage for the first time. Mullaghbuoy, Population 15, had been too small a burg to support any kind of theatre and any child expressing interest in play-making as opposed to scripture would be thrown off the cliffs as a danger to the community.

Wearing a cravat on the streets of Belfast could get you beheaded and the joke was that the church which dominated everything was against sex before marriage because it could lead to dancing – an even bigger sin. It was no joke, though. Life was real and life was earnest there and the grave was indeed its goal.

I was – and remain – a lousy actor but at once I understood that a stage was somewhere amazing things could happen. Remember the Dodgem Cars at the fair? They were connected to what always seemed to be a pretty ramshackle electrically charged metal ceiling by a pole that gave off a constant pop and snap of discharges accompanied by burstings of sparks and alarming blue smoke.

A whiff of something like cordite hung in the air – or was it brimstone? The stage was potentially a space like that, I instantly saw, where you could see characters bounce around like the miniature cars; colliding with each other, just missing each other, trapped in the arena of their passions until the ride was over.

*

When I saw that stage I knew I had to write for it and that's what I did for many a long apprentice year without getting anywhere except collecting enough rejection slips to paper the walls of Buckingham Palace until I turned into a dark alleyway one night and nearly got blown up by a bomb. A member of an Active Service Unit of the Provisional Irish Republican Army was planting it outside the telephone exchange halfway along it.

In an own goal the bomber blew himself up, his identity being later established by the prints on his thumb which was found on the roof of a pub fifty feet away. Had I turned into that alley thirty seconds earlier bits of me might have been decorating the city center too and these words would be coming to you via a medium.

The dead man would not even, in all likelihood, have accepted that I was Irish, despite the fact that I'd been born and raised there. He'd have been a believer in a Republican, united Ireland that had no place in it for people like me, whose ancestors were Scots and claimed a loyalty to the Crown.

It's an old quarrel and an old wound and here was my Rosebud, a personal issue to explore at a violent junction of history, religion, ethnicity and tribalism. In writing about it I found my voice and found it to be an Irish one.

My settler ancestors had been in Ireland for at least three hundred years and had been a tough bunch. Theodore Roosevelt wrote about those of them who moved even further West to settle in America — *'A grim, stern people, powerful for Good and Evil; relentless, revengeful, suspicious, knowing neither truth nor pity, for all his many faults the Protestant Ulsterman was of all men the best fitted to conquer the wilderness.'*

He meant those to be compliments, God help us but you get the idea. What was I to do? Deny those inconvenient ancestors? Celebrate them and turn a blind eye to the warts?

My response was to roll up my sleeves, start all over and write about my responses to that bomb, over a number of projects on stage and screen. Fortunately no one had given me the usual advice to writers starting out – to write about what you know.

I write that phrase with horror at the damage it has inflicted over the years. It has been as big a catastrophe for literature as the burning of the Library of Alexander (48 BC. Police are seeking a Mr. Julius Caesar to help them in their inquiries).

The fact that it's dished out either in Ignorance or its ugly sister Laziness is no excuse. The plain fact is that most people don't know much and what they know is odds-on likely to be banal and boring.

Unless you were born with three arms in the torpedo hold of the nuclear submarine your father built out of cheese and spent your early years inside it imprisoned in a Venusian space-port under the North Pole ice cap, forget it.

Don't write about what you know. Write about who you are.

The first is journalism. The second, art. And that's the fish we're frying.

5

SPANKARAMA

The person who talked more practical sense about dramatic structure than anyone I ever met edited porn movies. I met her when I first arrived in LA. She was trying to establish herself as a film editor in the legit world. Based in Van Nuys, where the movie stars and studio honchoes park their jets and which was also the center of the porn industry, she was trying to obtain her union card.

Like many others in Sin City she was learning her trade in the mis-named Adult Entertainment Industry but as a technician and not a performer. She understood to her fingertips that

DRAMA IS THE IMPACT OF EVENT ON CHARACTER

and nowhere is that rule more starkly in operation than on the porn movie set. Here is narrative reduced to its literally barest essentials – two or three actors, a storyline and physical action. Now and again there's dialogue but the silent movies proved you didn't even need that. In the editing suite she had to take the raw – sometimes extremely raw – footage and assemble it into a coherent shape.

Over the time she'd been doing this she'd learned that it wasn't enough just to show physical action, although in the end that was the point of it. There had to be some kind of narrative explanation for the gardener or window cleaner or pool boy to spot the sun bathing housewife or bored schoolteacher or nymphomaniac nurse in the shower.

It was usually the most tenuous of excuses for a storyline but a storyline it was. It just wasn't possible to show the act of sex taking place without any context and that context had to have movement in time, one of narrative's essentials, and a sketch of character, no matter how perfunctory.

What she learned in her studio apartment in Van Nuys would stand her in good stead come the day she got her union card and the right to work on network TV or in features. It was fascinating and instructive to listen to her expert analysis of what she'd seen in the movie theater or on the previous night's TV.

Just as porn can't just be a series of sexual positions, no matter how energetic, so a cops-and-robbers show, for example, can't consist only of gunfights. Her belief was that we were hard wired to want to watch other people have sex but that we were also hard wired to require deep story structure. This applies to *Hamlet* as much as *Around The World In Eighty Lays*.

The panting viewer, expectant hand on zipper, had paid good money for, in those days, the video cassette or CD, to see handsome young people getting it on but first it had to quickly be established who they were and how they met.

Once that was set up, the dramatic event had to follow, but as DW Griffith found at the dawn of the popular movie age, you have to make the audience laugh and make them cry but you also have to make them wait. Only then can you take them to the climax; whether it's a thousand people in the movie theatre or the lonely traveler in his (or her) sad motel room at midnight.

*

My only other (I swear) involvement in the porn world was set, oddly enough, in provincial England where I was approached by an entrepreneur who had a problem. He was the owner of a small video studio making instructional tapes. Business wasn't good. Salvation seemed to come when he was approached by a bent detective acting as middleman for a group of professional men in London who thought their monthly social evenings would be enlivened by the screening of dirty movies.

Not just any dirty movies. These were all ex-public school boys who had developed a taste for physical chastisement after Lights Out in their very exclusive dormitories.

It seemed easy money. The studio owner had committed to provide a thirty-minute movie based on the outline they sent him each month. They specified the type of girl required – blond, brunette, redhead – and a character type – schoolgirl, nun, traffic warden – and the implement she would be spanked with – tennis racket, warming pan, Cumberland sausage.

Their rules were strict – they were respectable and well regarded men after all and not perverts. The contact was to be little more than a gentle pat on the backside and should not leave any marks behind; even a faint redness was out. The spankee was never to be restrained but had to be seen to enjoy the mild chastisement. Nudity was *verboten*. In fact, it was the kind of thing you could have shown your maiden aunt, if she had a taste for mild flagellation.

*

My prospective employer's problem wasn't getting the actors. The bars and nightclubs of his city seemed to be teeming with people prepared to wield the implement or submit to it. What was driving him nuts wasn't the five minutes of spanking which was all the clients required but the twenty-five minutes of dialogue that led up to it.

It was, he had begun to realize having made a couple of these things, a terribly long time for his amateurs to improvise. There are directors who work in the improvised tradition, some with great success like Mike Leigh but he's working with actors chosen for their openness to the technique and backed up by his own commitment to it.

One could hardly expect Marlene or Darren, propositioned in a noisy nightclub with the offer to make a few quick quid, to suddenly become fluent in the form's demands. (On the subject of remuneration I was struck by the fact that the person on the receiving end was paid half what the person whacking them was.)

The offer to me was to write the dialogue for each episode. It would also be great if I knew any professional actors who would oblige. I said that few of them would think it a smart career move. It wouldn't have been a good one for me, either. I was at the time Writer in Residence at the Royal Shakespeare Company and recruiting prospective porn stars in the Green Room of the Memorial Theatre, Stratford-upon-Avon, would have raised eyebrows.

Promising to think it over, I left as soon as I could, having become aware that I was the only person around the table not armed. I never contacted the guy again but here was confirmation that structure mattered in every attempt to tell a story.

This applied even to the simplest stories of all, jokes. I learned this in the several weeks I spent working as dresser for a comic whose circuit were pubs and working men's clubs in the Black Country. He toured with a stable of strip-tease artistes and suggested I might get some material by traveling and working with him.

*

It was a tough gig because what he didn't tell me was that part of my job was to keep the girls safe, especially in the mining areas we played.

There had been a couple of 'incidents' and the comic was getting too long in the tooth to indulge in punch-ups with pitmen.

There were some touch-and-go moments but in reality the ladies could take very good care of themselves. Especially the star turn, who could have emptied a bar by herself, if things got ugly. She stands out in my mind because of her stunning, perfect body and the fact that she was sixty-three years old.

She had been forty years on the circuit, collected Georgian silver and was planning to retire to the Cayman Islands at sixty-five. She had a posh Solihull accent which added piquancy to the stream of curses she leveled at the horny-handed sons of toil in the front row who made the mistake of trying to grope her.

On the long drives home, with the girls asleep in the back seats, the comic would talk about the mechanism of jokes. *A man goes into a bar.* What is that but in miniature the narrative and character opening of every play or screenplay ever written?

He also claimed that his career had lifted off when he read that Charlie Chaplin had said you can't be funny unless your boots are too tight. At his next gig he had worn a pair too small for him and had the room in an uproar.

Could I have learned any of this had I the misfortune to go to Film School or had a charlatan's HOW TO WRITE WRITING manual pressed into my hand? One can never rule anything out but I doubt it. I learned the rudiments of dramatic structure not as theory but from the experience of those who needed to use it to make their rent.

Maybe not as valuable in the long term but certainly vitally necessary in the short term was the lesson in how to get out of a Miner's Club Dressing Room, across the car park and into the getaway vehicle, with strippers, comic, props and the booking fee in sixty seconds flat.

One never knows when that knowledge may come in handy again, one day.

6

SHE'S NOT LISTENING,
SHE'S BORED

When your head hits a book and there's a hollow sound, it might not be the book that has nothing in it.

Hegel.

You're going to have to hope that there's something in your script but how do you know that? Who's going to confirm it for you? Your boy/girlfriend wife/husband or maybe just a group of buddies whose opinion you would value spring to mind. You print a copy up and bashfully hand it to them and they say how excited they are to read it and – *are you nuts? Are you really intending to do that?*

If they're not professionally involved in the business what can tell you about it that you can value? You wouldn't hand them your chest X-ray and ask what they make of it. Put that crack pipe down. Reflect. Much as you love and admire them, your loved ones and closest acquaintances are the Great Unwashed when it comes to being qualified to help you. Are they really going to be honest if they think it stinks? Risk your friendship? End the relationship?

The closer they are to you the more unfair is the position you're putting them in. What you want, as all artists want, is to stand under, in Jonathan Miller's phrase, a waterfall of praise. If they can't give that is it their fault or yours for putting them in an impossible situation?

It was said of the marriage of the English historian Thomas Carlyle to his wife Jane that God put them together so that two people could be unhappy instead of four. Even that legendary horror show of wedlock would have been yet more unsupportable had either of them asked the other to comment on the action thriller, sitcom or romantic comedy they'd just completed.

*

If this has been a work for hire you'll have a producer or executive to report to and they'll tell you where you've gone wrong in no uncertain terms. Sometimes in the real world, however, that reading is done by the decision-maker in less than optimum surroundings.

This was borne into me on a flight on a now deceased but legendary airline, MGM Grand Air, which for a couple of years in the 1990s was the preferred mode of travel between LA and New York if you were a notch lower in the totem pole than those who had a private plane.

This was a period in which Steve Ross' dictum that if you looked after the Talent, everything good would come to the studio, held sway. That even extended to writers. In those years I believed that there was no way to get to the airport except by stretch limo. As we lived in an up-and-coming but still pretty marginal part of the city rumors probably spread that, from my mode of transport, I was a major drug dealer or a mortician.

MGM Grand Air had its own terminal on the other side of LAX and flew 747s converted for the use of a maximum of twelve passengers, in their own individual cabins. This was way beyond anything you'd ever get in even the most *luxe* of First Class anywhere else and the clientele were almost exclusively from the entertainment industry. They expected, as I came to expect, a standard of pampering which would make the Romanovs blush.

46   CLINGING TO THE ICEBERG

The treatment didn't end when the plane touched down at Kennedy because on several occasions I deplaned to be escorted to a waiting helicopter and whisked to the Hamptons on Long Island for a TV festival or meeting. Naturally another limo was waiting at the other end to take me to my rented beachfront gaff and the driver would be on standby all the time I was there.

Those days have gone with Steve Ross's passing and the corporatization of the industry and concomitant rise of the bean-counters but they sure were fun while they lasted.

*

On one of the flights a fellow passenger had to be helped into his seat, having drunk too deeply in the hospitality lounge before boarding. After we took off he consumed a cellar's worth of booze, burst into snatches of song, bounced around the aisle like a cork when he tried to find his way to the bathroom and finally drank so much that he passed into a catatonic sleep or death.

An hour or so later I passed his cabin and looked in. A screenplay was in front of him. He was making notes on it with a steady, certain hand and seemingly total concentration. On those notes would depend the future of the project, the author's reputation and, likely, a life-changing alteration in his financial affairs.

*

It's claimed that the ancient Persian monarchs made all their important decisions drunk and if they still felt the same way the morning after, when they sobered up, that decision stood. Perhaps this executive felt the same. If the ancient Persians got it wrong, of course, they would pay with their heads. Pretty much the same fate was waiting for the exec, come to think of it, if the project turned out to be a turkey.

Maybe he'd learn he'd been fired the way a producer friend of mine found out; when his key card wouldn't operate the security barrier at the studio gate. He wound the window down to point the malfunction out to the security guard who always had a cheerful word for him.

Not today. *You were fired last night, buddy,* the guard said coldly, checking his clipboard. *Make a U-turn and leave the lot.* He did so in shock and the next time he was allowed onto the premises it was in the company of two security personnel who waited with him until he'd cleared all his possessions into the Cardboard Box of Doom.

Labour relations have always been, shall we say, robust in Hollywood, with pitched battles a feature of the attempts to unionize the studios. I worked at Sony in the days before the ubiquitous cellphone. The first clue that somebody important was being fired was when the central switchboard was closed down so that no calls could be made in or out. This ensured the studio got its message circulated first. The second clue was the searching of all cars exiting the gates.

It's a little harder to police a workforce in the internet age but paper files are still important. Especially if they contain sensitive information about, say, a hot script or talent which might be persuaded to follow a departing executive to new pastures. The most spectacular cases involve agents with itchy feet.

Item from *Variety*, April 3rd, 1995 –

> *At 6:45 p.m. on Tuesday, March 28, David Greenblatt, the 40-year-old acting head of International Creative Management's motion picture literary division, sat in his boss's office discussing his future with the agency. The*

cordial meeting between ICM president Jim Wiatt and Greenblatt ended with the lit agent saying he hadn't yet made up his mind about whether or not to stay at the agency.

Later that night, a junior agent at ICM called his superiors to report that Greenblatt's assistant was removing files from the Beverly Hills office. ICM chairman Jeff Berg drove down to the office at midnight. Greenblatt and three other agents whose assistants had also been caught in the act of cleaning out their offices were dismissed. Thus was born the Endeavor agency. By the weekend, sources close to Endeavor estimated that the quartet had secured well over 50 of their former clients.

An analogy to military coups in Banana Republics might come to mind except the studios, networks and agencies have far more money than even the most vigorous kleptocracies. In full disclosure I have to note that I was an ICM client at the time and later an Endeavor client. I followed my features agent to the ominous, oddly kidney shaped corner building they then occupied on Wilshire Boulevard.

Wilshire regards itself in every way as Los Angeles' Main Street, running as it does from downtown, through Beverley Hills to the ocean. It's named after Henry Gaylord Wilshire, who sold the city the land for the first municipal dump in exchange for the property rights to what was an old Tongva Indian trail. The trail was also used by the early Spanish settlers and runs past the La Brea Tar Pits.

Many years ago pitch welled up from deep underground to form swamps. They're still there today and every so often belch out huge gobs of methane alongside the LA County Museum. Over the years literally thousands of animals wandered into them and got trapped – saber tooth tigers, giant sloths, mammoths and mastodons.

Struggle though they might, predators and prey alike, they found it impossible to free themselves and sank deeper with every effort to get out. I keep thinking there's a metaphor there for something but I'm darned if I can see what it is.

*

The only way to develop a tactile feel for your script – which is also another way to load it into your subconscious – is to read and re-read it at every stage of its making. Unlike visual artists – or the Disney animators – we can't step back and look at the quarter or half completed canvas.

I suggest that your reading is done not at that Louis Quinze gilt and ormolu desk you've bought on the expectation that your script is going to sell for a million bucks but that now's the time to get out of the squat and go to Starbucks. Or a bar. Or the nail salon. Take the pages with you and read them there. Read them not where the only sound is the whirring of the delicate mechanism of your own brain, but where there's distraction such as piped music or natter.

*

For some years I read in the noisiest Starbucks I could find, in South Central Los Angeles where there was a constant stream of potential distraction. A local pimp ran the morning and afternoon shifts of his 'girls' from one corner table; another was occupied by the Afghan owners of a hot-bed motel across the street who kept an eye out for Vice Squad raids from this vantage point.

Frequently cops would rush in, guns drawn, in hot pursuit of one of the local crackheads who had stuck up the tile store next door.

How much money is usually kept in the tills of inner city tile stores? Not a huge amount, I'd guess but this one seemed to be on the To Do List of everybody with a habit and a Saturday Night Special in Los Angeles.

I remarked on this to someone who believed I was exaggerating and who arranged to meet me there for coffee. We had front row seats for another tile store stick-up and chase and a bonus in the sudden entrance of not one but two seven-foot-tall men in African tribal robes who roughed up the pimp and left without saying a word.

My friend was persuaded but wait, I told him, there's more. This was the daily moment when the catheter of the guy in the wheelchair, a regular who had been paralyzed in a gang shootout, was changed by his helper. At the table. In plain sight.

Sometimes these often-baroque events would have me lift my head from the page. If they didn't I could feel pretty sure that the script was working; that the energy in my brain had burned like lava down my arm to my fingertips and delivered the ideas in it hot and smoking to the page.

Writing's a work-out. For the mind, spirt and body. Don't cheat it.

*

What follows are some of the things you're looking for when you read each draft. A stern warning. This is not to be read as a checklist, a series of mechanical actions to be ticked off. It's a cloud, a swarm of suggestions put deliberately in no particular order.

The process of creation is messy, with mis-steps and false starts. It's partly about your brain but it's also about gut instinct which you'll develop as you write. There are intestinal flora in the gut which react to stimuli faster than the organs of consciousness.

That's why we say we feel things in our gut and I can confirm for you that one of my tests when I read a draft is whether my stomach is unsettled. When the writing goes wrong I literally feel my skin prickle and my temperature rise. In time you will be as attuned to the material as that.

The following are the things I watch for as I endlessly re-read my drafts. Sometimes quietly to myself, sometimes playing the characters. I do this not as an academic exercise but because they will help in going forward to the next draft. Anyone treating them as a tool for analysis will be escorted from the premises.

DOES A SCENE SEEM TO GO ON A BEAT TOO LONG?

ARE ALL THE SCENES OF THE SAME LENGTH SO THERE'S NO RHYTHM TO IT?

DOES A CHARACTER YOU LOVE HAVE TOO MUCH TO SAY FOR THEMSELVES?

ARE YOU ASSUMING THE READER/VIEWER WILL LOVE HIM/HER JUST AS MUCH AND COULD YOU BE WRONG?

DO THE JOKES WORK?

ARE YOU TRYING TO DO IN DIALOGUE WHAT THE CAMERA WILL DO WITH VISUALS?

IS WHAT YOU THINK YOU ARE SAYING ACTUALLY ON THE PAGE?

ARE YOU CLEAR-EYED ABOUT THE DIFFERENCE BETWEEN WHAT HAPPENS IN A SCRIPT AND WHAT IT'S ABOUT?

ARE TWO CHARACTERS TRYING TO DO ONE CHARACTER'S WORK?

DOES A LEAD TO B AND B TO C SO THAT THERE IS A CHAIN OF CAUSE AND EFFECT FROM BEGINNING TO END?

DOES WHAT HAPPENED IN SCENE THREE PAY OFF IN SCENE NINETY-FIVE OR IS IT JUST THERE BECAUSE YOU'RE TOO LAZY TO STRIKE IT THROUGH?

COULD YOU PUT THE SCRIPT ASIDE AND TELL IT FROM MEMORY IN ONE GO? IF YOU TRY THAT AND KEEP STOPPING ARE YOU WILLING TO EXAMINE WHY YOU HIT A HICCUP? COULD THAT BE BECAUSE THERE IS NO INNER STRUCTURAL LOGIC SO IT'S THIS PAGE, THIS SCENE, THIS LINE WHERE IT'S ALL GOING WRONG?

HAVE YOU UNDERSTOOD THAT THERE'S REAL LIFE TIME AND MOVIE TIME? THAT ONE OF THE JOYS OF WRITING FOR THE SCREEN IS THAT YOU CAN MANIPULATE TIME, COLLAPSE IT, AND EXPAND IT BUT THAT ONE OF ITS MISERIES IS THAT EVEN WITH THE DIFFERENT CONVENTIONS OF MOVIE TIME (THE FLASHBACK, THE FLASH FORWARD, THE REPRISE) YOU ARE LOCKED INTO A LINEARITY? THAT IS, YOU CAN ONLY HAVE THE VIEWER FOLLOW ONE DARN THING AFTER ANOTHER AND THAT SPLIT SCREENS NEVER REALLY WORK AS AN ATTEMPT TO GET AROUND THIS?

ARE YOU CLEAR THAT THE SCREENPLAY IS SAYING JUST ENOUGH TO GET WHAT YOU SEE, LITERALLY SEE AND HEAR, LITERALLY HEAR INTO THE HEAD OF THE PERSON WHO IS GOING TO READ IT? THAT YOU HAVEN'T MISTAKEN IT FOR AN ESSAY OR SHORT STORY OR NOVEL WHICH MUST BE COMPLETE IN ITSELF ON THE PAGE? THAT IT'S OKAY, INDEED NECESSARY, TO HAVE LOTS AND LOTS OF

WHITE SPACE

ON

THE PAGE

because otherwise the eye is wearied and your characters are talking too much and keep on talking and talking and talking and talking and talking and talking and talking and talking and what the reader wants to know is what is going to happen next?

As in happen. As in event. Because if drama is indeed the impact of event on character you need to have an external event pressing on their inner life and you are going to need your character express what has happened to them in some externalized, physical way.

*

All that the reader of a script knows of a character is what they see on the page. Make sure they see it clearly. Use your hands on the keyboard to get it out of your brain onto that page. You have room in the early drafts to experiment but by the time the screenplay is ready to be shown to those who have paid for it, decisions should have been made.

These decisions are ones you should be able to defend because you should know who every character is, how they react to the other characters and what they would do and not do in a given circumstance. You should be able to point to the exact line and word on the page where that is demonstrated.

Delicate readers are advised to skip the next sentence but this is such an important note that it needs to be expressed with vigor. It's a Belfast street phrase relayed to me by producer Eoin O'Callaghan –

YOUR CHARACTERS CAN'T BE STUCK UP THEIR OWN
BACKSIDES PICKING BLACKBERRIES.

*

The only time I really lost it in the classroom was when I asked one student why a character who acted one way in scene thirty-five performed the opposite action in scene forty-two. The answer was that they changed their mind.

It was at that point that I threw the marker with which I had been diagramming out the sequence of scenes and let out a scream that surprised even me. I wasn't intending to hit the offender and if I had there'd be a million-dollar lawsuit coming down the pike but it got the point across.

Characters can't just change their minds like that. Not unless we see what has brought them to the inflection point and it has to be more than whim. Or, more likely, without the writer thinking through the emotional and narrative logic of the tale.

The hurling of the marker was a distant echo of how I used to be in my drinking days, when the fuse was shorter and the contents more combustible. I once picked up a rather stockily built director and threw him through the fire doors of the theatre.

I was protecting the lead actor, whose voice was going to be damaged by his being made to go through the forty-page speech which opens my play, *Rat In The Skull,* time after time with no notes given him.

The actor begged me to step in but the director told me to mind my own business. The producer was reluctant to get involved. Figuring that we needed an actor who could do more than sign his way through the extended opening aria I decided my loyalty was to him and the play and not the director.

Ultimately whoever pays the piper calls the tune but the corollary of that is that whoever is calling the tune should know what they're doing and cross no professional lines.

*

On one feature I was been asked what I thought of the rewrite done by the director on my script without my knowledge. The new script was whisked out in front of the producer and the director clearly thought it would be a *fait accompli*. The problem was that my name was on the title page and would remain there in the studio's files and become part of my record as a writer.

When I read the pages I responded that in all honesty it looked as if it had been attacked by a blind man with a hedge trimmer. I always thought *He jumped up and down in rage* was just a lazy literary phrase but if you rile people sufficiently they will turn red in the face and do a little jig.

That's what the director did and there followed what the diplomats call a full and frank exchange of views and eventually we got back on track.

I would write the movie. He would direct it. There was no point in me handing over a next draft that he could not, in all conscience, show to the producer or the actors. How to proceed?

The least useful note anyone can give you is *I don't like this scene.* Some women like bald men with big teeth. Others don't. You can debate the subject for days and make no progress. Statements such as that are expressions of personal taste and prejudice. They may be valid but won't move the ball forward.

What's needed is a mechanism to get to the objective rather than subjective. This keeps the drama on the page and not in the director's trailer or the script conference room or the five-star hotel restaurant. It's your characters who should be having the rich, exhausting emotional lives and crises and not you.

Ask if you can take two minutes to tell them

WHAT YOU <u>THINK</u> YOU WROTE

and then ask them

and listen closely without defensiveness. Often this simple catalogue of fact – where the scene took place, who's in it, what they say, how it's indicated they say it, where the narrative stood at the top of the scene and where it stands at the end – will lead to a breakthrough.

You'll realize maybe that you've been reading across or over or under your own text. What you *assume*, that is, is on the page rather than *what's actually there*. A simple example would be if a character, in your head, was speaking ironically and you hadn't given an indication of that in a stage direction.

If that doesn't fix it, again without heat or defensiveness ask

What do you think <u>should</u> happen in the scene?

This has the advantage that your interlocutor has to make some decisions, too, which allows you to select the words which ultimately will be pinned to the page.

My attitude as somebody who pays the mortgage with my writing income every month has always been

Give the director and producer more of what they want and less of what they don't want until they're satisfied the script is ready to shoot.

This doesn't mean you're taking dictation. Rewriting to a very specific brief is what writers-for-hire do. If you had fifty million dollars you could make exactly the move you wanted to but you probably don't. That means you have to pay more than lip service to this being a collaborative medium.

When you leave that meeting you will have genuinely taken on board the direction the new pages are to go in. You'll take pride in coming back with a scene which reflects the notes but also has a lot of you in it. You've been presented with a challenge and you've not undertaken it grudgingly.

Some of the most satisfying moments of my professional life have been wrestling with a difficult set of notes. What's helped me is an insight from a psychologist who said, of decision making that

SOMETIMES, IN ORDER TO CONCEIVE OF A THING AS POSSIBLE, YOU FIRST HAVE TO BELIEVE IT'S IMPOSSIBLE.

The very act of regarding it as something that can't be achieved places it in the category of things that have to be thought about in terms of whether they can be achieved or not. That allows that subconscious integration and synthesis to begin so it's worth spilling more ink to repeat that

THE SUBCONSCIOUS IS THE TRUE HERO OF THE IMAGINATIVE LIFE.

7

TWO MURDERS

It was while I was in conversation at the bar at Molly Malone's with the Irish actor who believed his bibulous exile was due to being double-crossed by Sean O'Casey that I received the phone call from the FBI. You don't forget things like your first call from a Special Agent. Especially when that call is in connection with not just a murder case but one with such political significance that it crossed the threshold to assassination.

The call came early in my time in Los Angeles. I was still learning my way around the city, the industry and my own strengths and weaknesses as a screenwriter. Many of those were a reflection of how I'd got there. Not via the usual route, by Film School or family connection. I'd had a job which had taken me down some mean streets where murder wasn't uncommon. Now one had caught up with me six thousand miles away.

I would head to the bar on the corner of Fairfax and Wilshire around eight and stay until two or three in the morning, liberated from the licensing laws back home. Nobody fell header over heels for the Boulevard of Broken Dreams than me and not just because of how relaxed those laws were here.

It didn't mean that I automatically fitted in or adjusted my basically Irish drinker's habits or affect to accommodate it. Brian Dennehy, the screen actor and also Tony winning stage actor insists, for example, that when we met there in 105-degree Fahrenheit heat I was wearing a creased raincoat and very odd shoes.

I think he's wrong about the raincoat but plead guilty to the shoes. Living in Murder City UK there were few places to stylishly kit myself out for what would be only my second trip abroad and to the entertainment capital of the world, at that.

The staff in Marks and Spencer put me into a heavy woolen suit with a white plastic belt; a striped polo neck sweater in nylon and shoes that had what I can only describe as a quilted effect. The high shine of the plastic they were made from brought the footwear even more attention.

There are few more fashion challenged than the working-class Irish. We need as a nation to be told that a six-pack of Guinness is not a fashion accessory. It only dawned on me that I must have looked a right twerp turning up for rehearsal at LA's most prestigious theatre like that when one of the female members of the company insisted I accompany her to a men's store forthwith and replace it all. Especially the belt. And the shoes.

It was in my DNA to find a bar I could be comfortable in. Molly Malone's fit the bill. It was there I could be found every night, meeting the locals, scribbling *aides memoires* on beer-mats, picking up messages in the pre-cellphone age and sinking pints. The Englishman's home may be his castle but the Irishman's office is his bar.

*

The phone call that interrupted the *craic* that night was concerned with the FBI investigation into the death of Allard K. Lowenstein, a longtime firebrand of the American left, who had been involved in every notable cause in the fractious 60s and 70s.

He'd been a leading critic of the investigation into the assassination of Robert Kennedy. I was staying in the same apartment Lowenstein stayed in when he was in Los Angeles.

I had been preparing to move out so that he could move in when I received a call from him, telling me not to bother as he'd been delayed in New York on some legal business. I thanked him and thought no more of the call until I heard on the car radio the next morning that he'd been shot in his office shortly after we hung up.

The call logs showed that I was one of the last people he spoke to. Thus the FBI's interest in me to arrange an interview and statement. There was nothing material I had for them – such as a confession – but it was a bit of a shaker.

I mentioned it when I got to the rehearsal and one of the theatre staff dropped her coffee cup and ran quickly out of the room when I said the name of the gunman. She and her husband had roomed with the killer in college.

From the outset of my time in Los Angeles, then, I was inclined to believe that things happened there and by extension the States, in ways they didn't happen in, say, Coventry or where I grew up in Mullaghbuoy.

That sense that I was in a wonderland for story-tellers grew when I was invited to the memorial service, based on my tenuous connection with the dead man. At that service I met Governor Jerry Brown, Linda Ronstadt, the members of the group Peter, Paul and Mary and many other activist-celebrities.

One man was pointed out to me as having stopped a bullet from the assassin Sirhan Sirhan in the Ambassador Hotel kitchen, along with the Senator. The bullet was lodged in too sensitive a place to be safely removed while he was alive but he had signed an affidavit to allow the Secret Service to open him up immediately on his demise to check the calibre.

Assassination, Conspiracy and Walt Disney's body the other side of the garden wall. What more could a story-teller want? I was further in Heaven when I discovered that the person who rented me the apartment had been on President Nixon's hit list and had a full set of the Watergate Committee appendices in her library.

Happy day! I spent hours poring through those volumes, which would make any conspiracy theorist's hair catch fire. One tidbit; in the early 1960s the CIA asked RAND (the Research and Development Corporation) to come up with a perfect surveillance tool in an open society. RAND had suggested tracking the citizenry by moving away from cash to a credit card based economy. If every transaction had a date, time and place on it – Bingo.

*

Let's add Paranoia to Assassination and Conspiracy to Walt's cadaver and throw in a hefty dollop of *real-politik,* US style. That was provided when the advance team for Edward Kennedy's final, as it turned out, Presidential bid, stayed in the apartment next door to mine.

They took to Molly Malone's like ducks to water. I got a first-hand view of the violence never far from the surface on a campaign when the Secret Service spotted somebody edging a little too close to Kennedy's rope line. Within seconds the edger was fifty yards away, his feet never touching the ground as two agents carried him off.

Later, at the bar with one of them he explained *Ted Kennedy lost two brothers already and we ain't gonna lose him too on my watch, buddy-boy.* So add Tough Guy Talk to Assassination, Conspiracy, the dead cartoonist and Politics and no wonder I never wanted to go home.

America was painted in bright, basic colors and if you lived here you would be taking part in something epic and extraordinary. My very first night in LA, after all, had been spent at the Bonaventure Hotel downtown during which a falling out over a drug deal led to the victim being dismembered in the shower on the floor immediately above me.

*

I'm an admirer of Thomas de Quincey who, along with Hazlitt, wrote some of the most perfect prose in English. de Quincey's 1827 essay *On Murder As Considered As One Of The Fine Arts* begins –

> *A good many years ago, the reader may remember that I came forward in the character of a dilettante in murder. Perhaps dilettante is too strong a word. Connoisseur is better suited to the scruples and infirmity of public taste. I suppose there is no harm in that, at least. A man is not bound to put his eyes, ears, and understanding into his breeches pocket when he meets with a murder.*
>
> *If he is not in a downright comatose state, I suppose he must see that one murder is better or worse than another, in point of good taste. Murders have their little differences and shades of merit, as well as statues, pictures, oratorios, cameos, intaglios, or what not. You may be angry with the man for talking too much, or too publicly but you must allow him to think, at any rate.*

If you don't want to rush to get the rest of his essay having read that, you're wasting your time contemplating a Life Among Letters. Reading on, you'll find de Quincey discussing the fatal deed considered from an aesthetic point of view. The British expatriate Raymond Chandler's essay *The Simple Art of Murder*, written in his own Californian exile, continues the conceit, in talking of the modern detective story.

Applying that yardstick, the murder/assassination of Allard K. Lowenstein, shocking and horrible though it was, doesn't quite live up to the murder of a man named Patrick Joyce in a Coventry traffic underpass some years previously, in the investigation of which grisly and surreal crime I had a supporting role.

This gave further evidence that the Gods of Comedy do run the world and that some of them have a very dark sense of humor indeed. Whatever your imagination invents isn't a patch on that cynical old plotter, Real Life. The victim in this case was also a man named Patrick Joyce so hang onto your hats. It could get a little complicated for a paragraph or two. You might even want to draw a diagram.

*

I was no stranger to violent death in the days when I was a home visitor for the Department of Health and Social Security. The mad, the sad and the bad were almost entirely our client list and my day consisted of calling on between a dozen and twenty of those in dire financial distress.

The poor, it has to be said, regrettably kill each other more often than anyone else. Ruth Gordon writes somewhere of the sour, brown smell of poverty and that was what was in my nostrils for most of my twenties. My beat was a large municipal estate containing the concrete barracks in which the poor were warehoused and the older and more squalid part of the city center.

The mad? One of my visits was to someone who locked me in the house after slipping out of the front door but not before he turned all the gas taps full on and lit a candle in the hopes of demolishing me along with the house.

Later that day he was found squatting naked in a tree throwing rocks at the cops and firemen trying to persuade him to come down. The sad? An ocean of those who lived those lives of sometimes not-so-quiet desperation from one welfare check to the next. The mad, sad and bad all together in one lump? – Patrick Joyce and Patrick Joyce.

Patrick One was found trying to saw the head off Patrick Two with a rusty hacksaw blade in a traffic underpass at three in the morning. Patrick One made no demur when arrested but refused to give a statement or throw any light on what, given the name of his victim, was either a complete coincidence or clue to a possible motive.

The police were therefore in that populous suburb Baffled. They came to me because the killer lived in a dosshouse which was on my beat and wondered if my dealings with him that could throw any light on the bloody and murky business.

*

These events were set not just in the Lower Depths but in the basement underneath the Lower Depths, into which few of my gentle readers may have stepped. It's worth taking a moment to establish this world, in which I once spent so much of my time.

The dosshouse was a ramshackle collection of old buildings in a side street with the mocking name Paradise Street. It was home to tramps and those who either couldn't pay the nightly fee at the Salvation Army Hostel or were too unruly to be admitted there.

My father stayed in it briefly when he first came to Coventry as a jobbing bricklayer and refused to talk about the experience. There were no chocolates left on the pillow at night, let us say. There might have been *something* on the pillow but not chocolate.

When I write *unruly*, I'm talking about those capable of creating a daily and nightly level of excitement far from the experience of most of us in our well-ordered lives. One who stands out is another Irishman who, when I first visited him, had one real leg and one artificial leg. The next time I had dealings with him the other, good, God-given leg had also been removed.

He told me, as if it was the best joke in the world, that he'd fallen down drunk in a park with the good leg in the water of a pond. Overnight it froze and he'd been too drunk to feel it until frostbite set in and it had to be removed, too.

Despite the fact that he was now a double amputee he caused so much trouble in the shebeens in the city that the police persuaded the owner of the dosshouse to hide his false legs when he looked particularly cantankerous.

This was a rough and ready world and each man and the few women in it hadn't much further to fall. If they did the Twopenny Rope was waiting for them. This was an even grimmer dosshouse nearby where there were no beds to sleep on but they could sit all night on a bench slumped over a rope. At six in the morning the rope was pulled away and off they went for another day on the stones.

Was there no graybeard among them who had wisdom gleaned from his rejection of the settled world? Indeed there was and he haunts me to this day. I spent a long afternoon with him as he fried his rashers in the Paradise Street kitchen communal pan and rewound his toe-rags on his feet.

Like the Russian Army, the knowing transient eschews socks for strips of cloth carefully tied between the toes, the only remedy for blisters, they claim, known to man. He told me that there was a circuit which he followed – Coventry to Lichfield, Lichfield to

Canterbury, Canterbury to York and several others and there were dosshouses like this in every one of them.

What all those destinations had in common was that they were cathedral cities. It was his belief that he was following a path first trod in medieval times and earlier, when the builders of those edifices travelled on foot with their tools and brawn in search of work. When that great age of faith and construction was over people like him, who couldn't abide a domestic life, still moved in that gyratory pattern.

If he was right here, in modern Coventry, the center of the British car industry, light manufacture and closing time punch-ups was an echo, a shadow, a footfall of the ghosts of five and six and seven hundred years.

*

There was none of this rough poetry in the life of either Patricks, who had both been about to slide from dosshouse to Twopenny Rope and the authorities were anxious to tidy the case up.

My interview with Patrick One had been in connection with his application for a new pair of shoes from the Shoe Fund whose coffers I tightly controlled. Appalling though it now seems, I had the authority to inspect the applicant's footwear and had life and death powers over issuing a voucher for a replacement pair of Size Twelves.

There was a steady, illicit trade in these vouchers, which were swapped at a discount for booze. The preferred tipple was hard cider mixed with cheap sherry. If that wasn't available, meths. And for those so far gone that not even meths touched the spot any more, metal polish.

I wouldn't try this at home if I was you but the idea is to filter it through a loaf of stale bread to get rid of the taste. What drips out at the end is just about possible to get down your gullet. If no bread is available you can strain it through your socks, shirt or underpants and many of the guys did that.

Both Patricks were, according to the dosshouse owner, desperately near that point. In which case they would sooner or later literally drown in their own blood, as one or two of his lodgers did every couple of months, when the alcohol wore away the wall of the arteries in their throat.

A vigorous smoker's cough would rupture them and the hapless man or women were goners. One of our present Patricks had helped the other avoid that awful death via vigorous use of the hacksaw and the question was why.

*

A feature of my interview with Patrick One had been the dosshouse owner telling me not to talk to his lodger directly. Patrick One had an invisible dog who accompanied him everywhere. If you wanted to ask a question you had to go through the dog, who spoke to him and only then would he reply.

This unusual arrangement had slowed the interview but stuck in my mind. Maybe the dog held the key? Off we trooped to that horrible Victorian jail in Birmingham, Winston Green, where the still silent killer was being held; myself, the dosshouse owner and the murder detectives. The guards, a bluff, insensitive lot, were vastly amused at these antics. Eventually we got the answers, via the dog.

Barred from every pub in the city, Patrick One was allowed by a barmaid at the Ring of Bells to nip in for a quick half when the gaffer was in the cellar attending to the kegs. Touched by her favor and friendship, Patrick One decided on a little joke to amuse her.

He would walk into the bar and ask for *One for me and one for my friend.* When she'd ask him where his friend was, he'd take a severed head out of a plastic bag, place it on the counter top and say *This is him.*

Smiles all around. We had the answer and the names were simply a statistical fluke, although Kafka might have had some fun with someone waking up in the cells to discover that they were being charged with killing themselves. Patrick One never did stand trial due to an insanity plea and I think even de Quincey would have agreed this was a doozy of a homicide.

*

For a writer nothing gets wasted and I've used bits of the world it was set in in many of my pieces, including my first stage play *Says I Says He* and in my adaptation of *The Captain of Köpenick*, adapted from Karl Zuckmayer's play for the vast Olivier stage of the National Theatre.

On a deeper level my experiences in those years led me to rule nothing out when inventing characters and situations. It wasn't just that I met a wide variety of my fellow men and women. Those I had met – desperate, broken or just batshit crazy – had been living so intensely that I had no reason to trammel the fictional ones I was creating.

The complications of their lives, the bad decisions they had made again and again were so baroque your jaw hit the ground listening to them. Given that, why censor the intricacies of invented plot?

*

At one time the endpapers of novels used to detail when and where they were written. *Bulawayo – Pskov – Pitcairn – 1939 – 1965.* Even if it was made up it showed that the writer assumed his or her readers would expect them to have travelled at least part of the world with their wits about them and notebook in hand.

Today the equivalent is too often a list of writing programs, bursaries and awards won. This dishearteningly suggests that the author has traveled from school to university or college and then into print in a sealed carriage with the blinds drawn, meeting only others like themselves.

The same trajectory too often applies to would-be screenwriters. The years spent in the Classroom are the years not spent on the *Wanderjahre,* the journeyman years when you travel and gain life experience.

The coin you bank in your twenties and thirties will be what you draw on in your writing life for years to come. You don't have to head off to the Alps or Tierra de Fuego to seek it but you do have to keep your eyes and ears open.

What you're looking for can be found down, say, an otherwise unremarkable back street in, say, Coventry. There an Irishman with no legs but a great yarn is waiting for you; or a graybeard who seems to have stepped out of an impossibly ancient England or a man named Patrick Joyce whose only friend in the world is an invisible dog and a barmaid who's taken pity on him.

Towards that Patrick Joyce is walking another Patrick Joyce and one early morning in a subway under possibly the most boring city in the United Kingdom their paths will cross and a great and improbable but true yarn will come your way.

*

Much of my television writing has been in the thriller genre. It's a great way for a writer to cut their teeth, imposing a discipline as rigorous as comedy writing. Instead of delivering a gag every half page, the thriller writer is required to come up with a reveal, reversal or plot twist.

No matter how deep the viewer is in their cheese dip, they'll notice when you cheat. An essential guide to the art of the thriller is Ross MacDonald who said

> IT'S NOT THE STRING AND IT'S NOT THE KNOT.
> IT'S THE UNTYING OF THE KNOT.

Too much tedious string of exposition and you lose the reader. Make the knotted mystery too complex and ditto. Allow them to be sometimes a step behind and sometimes a step ahead of you as you explain the darn thing and you have them. These are lessons to be remembered outside the thriller genre, too, of course, in their echo of Foster's majesterial command to *Only Connect*.

This still begs the question why I've been drawn to the genre. Not to every aspect of it, though. I won't take or try to sell anything to do with serial killers, for example. As a husband and father of a daughter – and also as a paid-up member of the Human Race – I refuse to add yet more cruelty and misogyny to the world.

Frankly, I despise my fellow writers who do. Not only on moral ground but because it's a lazy way to construct a narrative. As Von Stroheim said – *When the plot slows, torture the girl.*

On the other hand I won my Emmy for one of the first projects to deal with the reality of the Holocaust in *Murderers Among Us – The Simon Wiesenthal Story.* Over dinner one night I was assailed by another writer who felt that any attempt to write about that horror was impermissible. I saw his point. There are complex moral and ethical issues about in any way risking any kind of normalization of Evil.

No film image can convey any percentage of the filth, agony and hellishness of the camps. Yet I not only stood by what I had done to bring Wiesenthal's story to the screen and a wide audience, a few years later I took on another Holocaust project in Robin Willams' *Jakob the Liar*.

*

I think it's pretty clear that for me constructing thrillers is a kind of sympathetic magic; a device which allows me to control the residuum of the night terrors which I suffered as a child. Even as a teenager I dreaded sleeping in the dark and always kept a knife under my pillow. Political violence, especially when rooted in ethnicity or tribalism is different in kind from more casual violence. It's part of the inescapable fabric of everyday life.

In writing about murder in a fictional context I can recapitulate those terrors in a safe space and control the fear, panic, dread and threat of physical harm which comes with them. Entangling the fictional players in a skein of narrative allows me to control events.

I'm in charge. Not the mob who threw the Catholics off that picturesque cliff; the fire raisers who burned down the house at the end of the lane; the gunmen who shot my uncle in the back; the kid who broke my nose my first day in England; the neighbors who knocked each other senseless and co-workers who tried to gut each other instead of the fish and in my life in Los Angeles, the killers who stalked those sunny streets.

As Goethe said, where there is much light, there is much shadow. I found both in Los Angeles.

8

UNEXPECTED LESSONS OF LOLITA

I t's impossible to read *Lolita* without thinking that Nabokov must have written it in one ecstatic rush, a fever of inspiration.

Dickens sometimes gives you the same feeling that his feet never touched the ground in some passages. There's a story of him falling down the stairs one night, candle in hand, interrupted in his writing. Picking himself up, he re-climbed the stairs and resumed his writing. When the maid remarked in the morning how extraordinary it was that the candle hadn't gone out in his fall he was genuinely puzzled. *What fall?*

Now and again we all get that kind of rush of blood to the head, when we are in The Zone and the rest of the world falls away. Surely that was how Nabokov gave us what seems more and more to be his masterwork in, unbelievably, his second language of English?

Not the case. The project tormented him through false start after false start and successive failures of nerve, in which he repeatedly put the book away, despairing that he would get it right, let alone fit for publication.

As you labor on the fifth or fifteenth or fiftieth rewrite of a scene or an entire script you can take some comfort from that. As also from the words of the person who ran the Jet Propulsion Lab in Pasadena for many years. They do really amazing work. One of my neighbors in Los Angeles worked there. One day I asked him what he did and he indicated his laptop. *I control one of the Martian rovers from this.*

When his boss was asked how she kept so many talented and potentially difficult people working to the best of their ability, she said she had come to realize that –

TRUE CREATIVITY LIES ON THE BORDERLINE BETWEEN
CHAOS AND DISCIPLINE.

Too much chaos and the thing will never cohere. Too much discipline and the juice is squeezed out of it. Thankfully your brain has two modes of operation. In one of them it goes into the world, looking for things to use in the creation of an imaginary one. In the other it sorts those things into boxes and discards whatever is immaterial.

That *yin* and *yang* between chaos and discipline; the trade-off between desire and technique is the tension which allows creation to happen.

*

Fine words but how do you balance them when you think you've handed in a pretty good draft and have to face a barrage of emailed notes? Or the summons to the conference room, where the intention is, you fear, to beat you and the script like a tethered goat? You've chosen to work in a collaborative medium after all so you can't shyly refuse to take part in this Western version of Chairman Mao's Self Criticism Session.

Better get used to it – script meetings are going to be part of your life and one of your professional requirements is the cast iron ass which will allow you to sit through them.

You'll usually be posed in a Herman Miller chair – the thousand-dollar ones with the webbing and shiny knobs that look like a praying mantis. In front of you is the conference table which will be anything between ten and thirty feet long and worth more than the car you drove here in.

My favorite was in Skydance, the offices of the people who produce Tom Cruise's movies and which is made from the wing of a Second World War bomber. Appropriate because in these sessions you'll take a lot of incoming fire.

As you survey those opposite you, all clutching those yellow legal pads which are their tools of office as development executives or director's hatchet person, you'll make a quick head count. There will be some very smart people here. One of the others, unfortunately, is certifiably crazy. One is totally deaf. One of them has no talent but has to be handled with care because they're sleeping with the studio head. The next one along (there can be a dozen people around this table) is a Yesser, agreeing with everything the brashest person in the room says.

There might even be somebody who hates you and you will have no idea who that is or why. Several years into my career somebody asked me what I'd done to piss off – for legal reasons we'll call him X. I said I'd never heard of X and certainly had never even been in the same room as X.

> *Well he's heard of you,* was the reply. *In fact, in today's staff meeting at the agency he said – and I quote – 'That fuck Hutchinson. I'm going to see that I destroy his fucking career.'*

X went on to be a very, very powerful player in Hollywood and I never did find out what I had done to upset him. Did it affect my career? Were there gigs I could have gone up for that never came my way? Impossible to know. Had I been mistaken for somebody who dented his BMW in the parking lot or comforted his wife when he was on the agency retreat? Likewise.

*

Before the ordeal begins there's the usual polite but joshing two-minute foreplay of inconsequential chit chat. It's a ritual as stratified as the Japanese Tea Ceremony and has the same function in establishing status. Status-defining topics include cars, boats, houses, tennis coaches, diet, divorce attorneys and vacation plans.

In one meeting the chit-chat turned to art. That resulted in an untoppable moment when someone asked the current wife of an eminent British creator of musicals who was present if it was true they'd just bought a Van Gogh. *We did,* was the reply. *But when we got it home we realized we'd bought the wrong one.*

I guarantee that I will never utter this phrase and nor will you but spare a moment in sympathy for the dismay of the billionaire couple who finally get the wrapping off the new purchase only to realize it doesn't go with the curtains.

When the two minutes of schmoozing are up the bell sounds for the first round. In one of these meetings, at Lifetime, I was slapped on the back and told I'd done a terrific job. *No, I mean it, Ron, a really terrific job.* The studio just had a few notes. Hardly any at all, really. But maybe they should run them past me, to see what their thinking was for the next draft. *Mary J Blige and Angela Bassett are booked and this is just the final dotting of the i's.*

Two hours later the spine of my notebook broke under the strain and my pen caught fire. Not really. But I had been given a total of seventy-eight notes, covering twelve closely written pages. Not all of them were biggies, I wasn't to think that.

The script really really worked and everybody loved it and this would be the last draft before the production draft. Oh and apart from the little notes there were four or five major ones. Say ten. Or make it a dozen. Or twenty. These were all headline notes and don't show us the next draft unless they're dealt with, sonny boy, or else.

They don't put it like that but that's their meaning. Fix these notes and your labor is at an end. As God's their witness you won't have to look at the script ever again. *This is it.* These seventy-eight notes are the very last word. *We'll be sending you a copy of these notes and we're done.* Except that there are also a couple of other things they'll be adding in there that they don't need to get into right now.

Scraping of chairs, more chit-chat, assistants sticking their heads around the door, anxious to chivvy their executives to the next meeting, *If you parked in the lot don't forget to get validated on the way out* and that's it.

Another day in Hollywood and the execs head on to their next sixteen meetings and the ink stained wretch crawls back to the kennel to try to make sense of the notes. (Making sure before leaving the lot to get the parking ticket stamped with the validation because if there is one thing that makes people earning many multiples of the average wage see red it's having to pay five bucks out of their own pocket for parking.)

*

Some of the notes are simple. Some are so complicated that they would, if imaged, look like the wiring diagram of the Space Shuttle. Some seem to come from The Place Beyond Time. Often you are reminder of Wittgenstein's axiom that if somebody tells you two and two equal five, you have a problem but can still work with each other but if they say the answer is a hundred and ninety-seven, forget it.

Others again are what I think of as One Legged Chinaman notes. At some point somebody will point to a page in the script and say *This is where the one-legged Chinaman should come in.* Or will point to the same exact place and demand to know why you've written a part for a one-legged Chinaman. You will look in vain for any reason why a one-legged Chinaman should appear in the project or conversely any evidence that you have ever included one.

It sounds bizarre and it is but it's happened at some point on every single screenplay I've written. I don't pretend to understand it but it's an undeniable artifact of the process. Listen to this note. Nod sagely in response. Write down the words *Add One Legged Chinaman*. Or *Remove One Legged Chinaman*.

Look them in the eye and solemnly promise that the issue of the missing or intrusive imaginary Oriental will be dealt with as a matter of urgency. Then do nothing about it. By the time they read the revision they will have forgotten all about it and the project will stay on the rails.

The One Legged Chinaman is not to be confused with the situation in which the director or producer is actually referring to a different motion picture altogether. This happened when John Frankenheimer and I were getting increasingly baffling notes from Dino de Laurentiis.

We both loved the guy and in his inimitable growl he assured us he knew how to fix the movie. When he was called out of his office to deal with something else John flipped the script around to face us. Ours was a political thriller set in China. This script was another episode in the Hannibal Lecter saga.

Having been in Hollywood all his career, John knew how to deal with the situation. When Dino came back in, he said we were so excited by the notes that we wanted to leave immediately so that we could get onto them right away. Next time we met Dino had the right script and no reference was made to earlier events.

John was no shrinking violet. He treated directing as a contact sport. I often heard him respond to a producer's suggestion about, say, a budget issue with *You're confusing me with somebody who gives a shit* but not even he was going to embarrass the guy who wrote the check.

*

Even if the One-Legged Chinaman doesn't make his appearance you may be put in mind of the Russian peasant who sees an automobile for the first time. *Where are the horses?* he marvels.

The driver explains that an explosion of gasoline vapor caused by an electrical spark causes a piston to move inside a cylinder which turns a crankshaft and by means of a gearing system the transmission moves the wheels backwards or forwards creating motion. *That's amazing,* says the peasant. *Where are the horses?*

When confronted with a note like that you should be asking whether they want the script better or just different. Often they're not sure themselves. It might have been a note like this which had one writer refuse to even think about rewriting on the grounds that he wasn't so conceited as to think he was any smarter now than he was six months previously.

Just as in my boozing days I prided myself on being able to drink people under the table, so here I'm determined to *think* them under the table. But I'm going to be doing the thinking on that deeper level too, where integration and synthesis happen internally. I don't have to prove I'm the smartest person in the room. Just the smartest person on the page.

My attitude has always been that as a freelance writer I have an employer but as everyone on the other side of the table is on salary they have a boss. There's a very real difference. It's hard to convey the depth of the fear and panic that are the twin motors of the executive life. So much of their fate is outside their own control, depending on the talent, judgement and performance of others.

Two vignettes of someone I knew who ran a major network. In the first her day is divided into fifteen minute segments. In each of those she has several decisions to make in which she has final say. When she heads out of the office there will be three or four people buzzing around her, needing more decisions, handing her coffee, charging ahead to hold the elevator.

Driven to lunch or a set or location she'll be firing off memos and *ukases* like a fighter pilot dueling the Luftwaffe over World War Two London.

The second is after it all went South. She's in a coffee shop with far too much time on her hands. When I bump into her she flinches. The last thing she needs is to say Hi to somebody who knew her in her pomp. Conversation is awkward.

She shows animation when she gestures to the book she's reading. It would make a great movie. Give her a couple of weeks and she'll get in touch with me about adapting it. When the studio let her go, she was given an indie producing deal, after all. Sure, I say, knowing she isn't going to call me and if she does, I won't be calling back.

There's a legendary writer who clearly didn't share my lurking sympathy for the executives he had to deal with. He was known for assiduously putting things down in his notebook and expressing effusive thanks for the help he was getting.

When he accidentally left the notebook behind one time the execs saw that he'd written FUCK THESE USELESS BASTARDS several score of times. That's why he's now a legendary screenwriter and not a working one.

*

Does this mean that you have to take everything that's thrown at you and write stuff you don't believe in? No way. You have to work out the boundaries of your own willingness to accommodate them and refuse to budge if you think you're being asked to compromise your own ethical standards.

Case in point was when John Frankenheimer wanted me to write a new scene on the set of the Emmy-winning *Against The Wall*. It didn't matter what the scene was, as long as was expensive. HBO would then come back and say they were going to refuse to budget it, which would allow him to pretend to blow his stack and browbeat them into ponying up for more extras in a scene he *did* want to shoot.

I turned him down. Turning John down was not a thing you did lightly. This was our first movie together but I was mindful of all the stories about him. Including the one when he'd asked for a beat-up old Rolls Royce for a scene and instead had been delivered a gleaming new one, direct from the dealer's showroom.

John took a hammer from Props and smashed every window, head and tail lamp, finally throwing the hammer aside with *That's what I asked for.* He was also notorious for waking up sleepy extras by having the armorer fire off a few rounds from an AK-47 over their heads.

My name was on the screenplay, however and if they roll over you once, they'll keep rolling over you. John was incredulous when I refused. *I'm the director and I'm telling you to do it.* To which my reply was *I'm the writer and I won't do it, even if you threaten to fire me.* I meant that. You have to mean it. You have to be ready for them to check you out of your hotel and send you home.

*

In saying 'No' I was following on the tradition of old-time Hollywood writers from the Golden Age, who made a good living in the Writer's Bungalow but who could be put on suspension at a moment's notice. Each one of them knew where the line in the sand was drawn for them individually; the point beyond which they wouldn't go.

Some of them were shielded by their celebrity, like William Faulkner who asked during an impasse if he could write at home and when told he could, promptly decamped to the South, two thousand miles away.

Some were just as tough as the studio chiefs they were getting the paycheck from. Like Herbert Mankiewicz. When Harry Cohn boasted that he knew what the audience wanted in the seat of his pants, Mankiewicz said *Fancy that. The whole world wired to Harry Cohn's ass* and got fired – not for the first time.

Most of them were working stiffs, ex-newspapermen or East Coast playwrights or short story writers who had lucked out and would have to explain to their wives and children why they'd been suspended or fired, for making a stand.

A stand on that intangible and subjective thing, Principle. Which put at risk only too real and objective such items as school fees, alimony payments, the mortgage and, more likely in the Golden Age than today, the discreet apartment for the boyfriend or girlfriend on Wilshire Boulevard.

It was in that less squeamish age that Arthur Laurents, after all, defined an 'actress' as 'any young women in Los Angeles under the age of thirty-five not actively employed in a brothel.'

I turned John's demand for the rewrite down and he accepted it. We went on to work together many more times. It was one of the most important professional and personal relationships of my life and I miss the guy every day.

The relationship was founded on his acknowledgment of moral choice that cynics, who have usually never spent much time out there, assume don't play a part in a Hollywood career; viewing everything through the lens of Budd Schulberg's rotter Sammy Glick or the Cohen Brother's sour Barton Fink.

*

It's not to be denied, however, that some of your experiences around the script conference table require a great effort to keep a straight face. Often they can be downright surreal. At one meeting on a projected international co-production of *War and Peace*, one of the producers asked for extra characters to be invented as he felt Tolstoy's masterpiece was a little light on them.

I don't think that's a charge that's ever been levelled at the heavily bearded Russian. The opposite from Western readers, if anything, who tend to get mightily confused by each character seeming to have three different names, plus nicknames. I parted from the project shortly afterwards and have no idea whether the screenwriters added a Chuck or a Tiffany to make the story more accessible to a modern audience.

Sometimes you'll risk whiplash and a dislocated jaw as you hear a note. That's what happened to me when my director on a Coco Chanel movie said firmly that the least interesting thing about her was that she designed clothes. I guess his Albert Einstein biopic skipped the science and concentrated on his career as a baseball umpire.

I also struggled to keep my deadpan when another director told me that he intended to shoot the movie with what he called 'circling camera motions'. This technique would require me to write in a similar way. My request for clarification was greeted by an impatient waving of his hands. *Circling motions. Like in circles.* Something may have been getting lost in translation so I went ahead and wrote it the way I always did. In straight lines. He never noticed.

The most startling thing to happen at any meeting was being asked to fly to one of the Gulf States to help collect a large sum of money promised to the production. It was felt that the project would be more real to the backers if a Hollywood writer was there.

Call me crazy but I have a natural caution about flying anywhere in the world to pick up what would have been several tens of millions of euros in cash. I was assured everything was on the level. Someone had loaned them his private plane and we would have protection in the shape of a close relative of the security chief of one of the Palestinian factions.

A tempting prospect! To be flown in the private plane of a mystery man perilously close to Israeli airspace with a bag of money guarded by somebody likely to be on everybody's watch list. A business plan or elaborate multi-suicide mission?

I declined and that project, like so many others, may have been made and is playing at a multiplex near you if you live in an alternative universe. It's certainly not playing in this one.

*

If you take one thing into script meetings take this note from Henry James which can help you keep your head when things are getting complicated –

> THE ONE THING THAT ARTISTIC TEMPERAMENT
> CAN'T CREATE IS ART.

I made sure that I remembered it in the dozens of meetings I took every year for thirty years. Although sometimes it was touch and go…

9

GETTING THE STORY
ONTO THE PAGE

George Bernard Shaw averred that the mark of a good play is that you can sleep through ten minutes of it and not miss anything that matters. The movies and television, alas, don't allow you that luxury. When I went to Los Angeles I was lucky to meet people who knew how to make every screen moment and every frame count.

One of them was the great writer, director and teacher Frank Pierson. His screenplays include *Dog Day Afternoon* and *Cool Hand Luke*. You don't get many of those to a pound. His story about how the latter came about gives heart to anyone who has written anything which seems to have sunk without trace.

After lunch with Paul Newman at Musso and Frank's on Hollywood Boulevard they were waiting for their studio cars and drivers, who had been delayed in traffic. Idly Newman picked up a ten cent book on a nearby remainder stall, flipped through it, said *This could be interesting* and handed it to Frank, who turned it into Oscar gold.

I met Frank after he used my screenplay for Brendan Behan's *The Hostage* in one of his screenwriting classes. Later we both taught at the American Film Institute. He believed that Hegelian dialectic was what movie writing was all about; one character speaks the thesis, the next the antithesis and from that interchange synthesis results.

The three-act structure is based on the same foundation. The first act says here is a problem to be resolved – a love affair, a crime, an impossible journey to be undertaken. The second act offers possible contending solutions – choose A or B instead of C, offer up various suspects who could have committed the crime and detail the differing routes the journey could take and their hazards. In act three true love wins, a mystery is solved and the journey is accomplished.

*

You will no doubt be aware of Maurice Merleau-Ponty's claim that *All the great philosophical ideas of the past century – the philosophies of Marx and Nietzsche, phenomenology, German existentialism, and psychoanalysis – had their beginnings in Hegel* and even if you don't you'll get the idea that Hegel's a bit of an intellectual bruiser who has to be taken seriously.

This is not the place for me to critique his *Phenomenology of Spirit* or explore my differences with him on the issue of Kantian dualism; mainly because I have no idea what he's talking about but I have found his statement that in order to create anything we have to –

BANISH THE WATCHER AT THE GATES OF THE MIND

– to be possibly the single smartest and most profound thing anyone ever said about how to get the courage to throw yourself into an act of creation and, once you've begun, not to lose heart by constantly second-guessing yourself and packing the whole thing in. He's encouraging us to plunge in and recklessly forge ahead like a drunk or sleepwalker.

Philip Larkin said that writing was, for him, a physical need. Let's say you feel that need, whether to get something political or deeply personal off your chest or because a character, a scene, a phrase is burning a hole in you, then nothing is going to stop you expressing it by smacking a blank page in the mouth.

When you have it, don't agonize. Get something down on paper. Think of a ski jumper. When the siren sounds they don't spend thirty seconds checking if their sunglasses are on properly or tapping out a final email. They launch themselves down the hill.

Your first task is to tell us where the first scene is taking place. This isn't a novel. The camera will do most of the work. All you need to do is describe in as few words as possible where we are, what the time of day or night is and who is in the scene.

Write what you want the characters to say. Remember that characters in movies and TV don't speak to each other the way we speak to each other in real life. Look at the difference between even the best actor improvising a scene and a newsreel. We accept a very different, highly artificial discourse on the screen which, at its finest, is a kind of lyric poetry.

It helps to be in love with how people actually speak in order to write words for your characters and when you do that you discover the different rhythms in even ordinary exchanges; there are long, uninterrupted word runs, a moment of quiet or hesitation, then another long run, this time an interrupted one, then a run of short, staccato exchanges or one word repeated a couple of times. When your scene is complete check to see what it actually looks like on the page.

If every character speaks in five line chunks of dialogue, identical page after identical page, you're sunk. Break it up. Pick up a pen with red ink. Score out everything that falls dead on your inner ear. Make sure there's lots of white on the page and not what looks like an unusually dense bit of Proust.

If there isn't white space, create it by hoovering out line runs at random and seeing if you even miss them. The great television writer Dennis Potter claimed that he removed the first three pages of every screenplay and lost nothing by it. You'll be surprised how far these seeming mechanical – almost arbitrary – adjustments can get you.

*

The job ahead now that you have your first location and set your characters yapping is going to be helped immeasurably if you have a story you want to tell and not just a world or theme to describe. You're looking for one hundred to one hundred and twenty pages and the final Fade Out is going to be a long long way from Tipperary unless you have a narrative to help you get there.

An example of the kind of narrative that does a lot of the work for you? A lawyer in Los Angeles told me about a guy on Death Row in Louisiana who went nuts waiting for his date with Ole Sparky. Barred from putting to death someone mentally ill the State hired a shrink to talk him sane so that he could be legally fried. I knew at once this was a Derby winner. It had everything. Milieu! Character! Moral conflict! The Electric Chair!

Every mechanical wristwatch is powered by a mainspring which as it unwinds, drives the entire mechanism and set of complications. A sliver of story like that is the tightly wound mainspring which will power one hundred or so pages. In this case it resulted in an HBO movie which won the equivalent of the Emmys for cable TV.

It was an interesting shoot, in a working jail in Montreal. At one point the sirens sounded and the guards started rushing around in an agitated manner. The place went into lockdown because in one of the cellblocks a genuine riot was taking place. A brief consultation and we continued shooting. It just costs too much to lose even a half day given the expense and time constraints of making a movie on location.

*

Assuming that you have the first scene and your characters are making sounds that resemble human speech and that you have a story to tell, don't rush to get to the end.

There's a performance anxiety which afflicts beginning writers, who aren't totally sure they can keep all the balls in the air. They feel the need to try to get to *Finis* as soon as possible, if only to see if the darn thing works but I'm going to give you an image that I shared with my AFI students, who found it helpful.

It's also an image I use every day of my working life, its value being in combining the subconscious with the practical. I told them to –

> Think of a screenplay as a big, creaking old house and every scene as a room in that house. Go into the first room. It's a little dim in there and hard to see across but you know there's a door in the opposite wall somewhere. Write your way to that door. Open it. You will see a second room. There is a door in one of its walls too. Write your way towards it. Find that door. Go through it. Do this for every room until you have written your way through the entire house, basement to attic. Do it one room at a time and if you haven't found the door at the end of each three hour writing session, leave it for the next day. Your unconscious imagination will in the meantime have been at work, exploring it and preparing to guide you when you return.

(This volume would contain many useful more tips like this, trying to teach story through story and image through image but the notebook I kept when teaching was stolen in Florence with much of my luggage by Moroccan terrorists. A long story, not without interest but its only place here to is indicate the source of this practical advice.)

10

SUNK COSTS

Part of your equipment as a working writer will be an understanding of what may seem, at first blush, to be an arcane economic theory. A mastery or even a rough idea of Sunk Costs will save you much time and heartache, not only in your professional life but personal and domestic. It's usually stated in the form of a fallacy –

> *When losses threaten on an investment further investment is warranted by the fact that the resources already invested will be otherwise lost.*

It's a fallacy because it doesn't take into account the further potential losses which will accrue when the original money can't be recouped no matter how much money you piss into the sand.

That's not exactly how the behavioral economists Daniel Kahneman and Amos Tversky put it in their Nobel Prize-winning papers but you get the idea. They said that *Sunk Costs often affect economic decisions due to loss aversion: the price paid becomes a benchmark for the value, whereas the price paid should be irrelevant... This has enormous implications for finance, economics, and securities markets in particular.*

It also has implications for the screenwriter when pressured to junk a page, a scene, an act, or an entire screenplay or stage play you have, you feel, spilled your heart's blood into and want to dig your heels in to keep. It's a more precise rewording of Faulkner's –

Slaughter your darlings

and the anonymous military man who directed his fellow generals to –

Never reinforce failure

or your mom's

There's no point crying over spilt milk.

The classic experiment in this field is of course that of Knox and Inkster. They approached 141 horse bettors: 72 of the people had just finished placing a $2.00 bet within the past 30 seconds, and 69 people were about to place a $2.00 bet in the next 30 seconds. Their hypothesis was that people who had just committed themselves to a course of action would reduce post-decision dissonance by believing more strongly than ever that they had picked a winner...

There's a lot more in that vein and no, I didn't follow a word of it either but Knox and Inkster were obviously the goods. If you need more, check out their academic work. The lesson for us is that it doesn't matter how many hours you spent on the pages you're being asked to junk.

In a very profound way they don't yet exist no matter how painful or painstaking their composition was. That DELETE button on your laptop or little bit of rubber atop your pencil have a reason for being there. Use them. They're your friends and not your enemies.

Either Rodin or Michelangelo (not sure which – the Research Department is closed for the day) said that making a sculpture was about removing the marble that blocked the view of the shape which was already locked in there. It's going to hurt sometimes to sacrifice dialogue, themes, devices, gags, thrills, clever-dick reverses and sometimes even characters but if they have to go they have to go.

Either because the red-faced producer is banging the desk with his loafer demanding it or the even more demanding writer inside your breast is telling you it has to happen. Of course there will be circumstances in which you feel that move is the wrong one but that feeling should never have anything to do with the argument that, golly gee, that stuff took hours and hours to write and by that very fact deserves to stay.

*

The most famous example of a producer refusing to fall for the Sunk Costs Fallacy was when David O. Selznick halted production on *Gone With The Wind* after three weeks of shooting. He wasn't happy with the way George Cukor was filming it. He wasn't happy with how the actors were playing it. He wasn't happy with Wardrobe. He wasn't happy with Production Design. Most of all he wasn't happy with the screenplay, even though it had cost him a fortune and he'd thrown the talents of seventeen writers including F. Scott Fitzgerald at it. Yes, that F. Scott Fitzgerald.

Aware that he was putting his career, fortune and relationship with his powerful and odious father in law, Louis B. Mayer on the line, he made the momentous decision to halt production until he had the screenplay re-written.

Even across the years one has to be in awe of his guts in giving the order. Stopping a movie in production is like stopping an air craft carrier at full speed ahead. Ignoring the pandemonium the decision was creating he summonsed Ben Hecht and Victor Fleming, the director who still had one third of *The Wizard of Oz* left to shoot and told them he was locking them in the room until they had a screenplay.

This was an era in which it was still possible to treat an A-list director as if he was on the janitorial crew. To do the same thing to one of today's *auteurs* would probably require a resolution from the United Nations Security Council.

Not even the hard charging Fleming could resist the edict. And this was a man who had not only slugged Judy Garland when she had a hysterical fit but was notorious for having shot a cat in the grounds of the Beverly Hills hotel that was disturbing his *amour* with one of his leading ladies.

*

What happened in the next five days occupies a page in Ben Hecht's autobiography *A Child of the Century* which, along with *Gaily, Gaily*, his memoir of the newspaper world in Chicago, is required reading, class. Hecht claims to have been at that time the only person in the US not to have read Margaret Mitchell's wonderful but very long novel.

His belief was that of most Hollywood insiders that nobody wanted to see a Civil War movie, instancing several recent flops. The two-fisted Fleming seems not to have cared what movie he was shooting as long as somebody put a script in front of him. Sensing his Boy Wonder title slipping away from him, Selznick, Hecht claims, locked the door and fed them a brain-enhancing diet of bananas and peanuts until the work was done.

It's also highly likely that Selznick consumed enough Benzedrine to power the entire field in the Kentucky Derby for at one point he passed out, stone cold, for several hours in such a deep sleep the other two wondered if he was dead.

Sensing the comic possibilities in this and wanting to write my Hollywood play after spending so much of my life there, I used this page as inspiration for *Moonlight and Magnolias*, which has toured the world, made millions of dollars and seems set to enter the repertoire.

The play is a love letter not only to my bank balance but to Hollywood. I loved that place the first day I got there and saw the palm trees waving at the studio gates. I never cease to get a kick when driving through those gates.

At a later stage I'll explain my moving to the East Coast but I still have deep affection for Los Angeles and its manifold craziness. Affection? Passion. Every love affair with the movies is doomed to disappointment, however, because whoever the Goddess of movie making is, she's pretty skittish with her favors.

I'm beginning to wonder though if the old girl isn't getting a little long in the tooth. When I first went there in the early 1980s there was still a very real snobbery against those who worked in television as opposed to those who worked in features.

That's totally changed now and not just because the lolly is spread around much more liberally when you write for the Idiot's Lantern than for the Silver Screen. Each TV show that goes into syndication is worth over a million dollars an episode, for example. Each year brings more evidence that the power of cinema is being supplanted by video games, online poker, tractor pulls, hot-dog eating contests and antisocial media.

*

One of the most telling proofs is that suggested by another part of the work of C. Northcote Parkinson, which notes that undertakings which are scrappy and successful as they battle their way to market domination have no time to spend building monuments to themselves. It's only when they are at the apogee of their power that they build themselves grandiose headquarters.

The day of the ribbon cutting ceremony at that headquarters is usually when their decline begins. He cites among other examples the George Gilbert Scott building in Whitehall, intended to house the central machinery of the British Empire, which opened in the year the Empire began to fall apart with upheaval in the Jewel in the Crown, India.

Since 1910, when the first movie was shot in Los Angeles, the industry managed to get along without a museum devoted to its own admiring reflection. Sure, there were the annual bun fights of the Academy Awards but everybody was so busy making money and screwing each other that there was no collective drive or deep-seated need to erect a temple to themselves and their art.

That temple is now being built on Wilshire Boulevard. The website that fronts the online begging letter for its construction costs reads *The Academy of Motion Picture Arts and Sciences is building the world's premier movie museum in the heart of Los Angeles. Located in the historic Wilshire May Company building at Wilshire and Fairfax, the Academy Museum will explore the history and magic of what happens on screen as well as behind it.*

Renderings of the structure show it sticking suggestively out of the side of what used to be the reconfigured department store I bought my first button-down-collar shirt from, a stone's throw from the Molly Malone pub.

No doubt it will be a successful addition to the other theme parks in Southern California but it will be commemorating a popular cultural artifact that is no longer central to the public imagination rather than celebrating one that dominates that imagination.

I can't believe the art form I so admire will go the way of the horse collar or gas mantle but the writing may well be on that improvised vertical writing surface, the wall. The members of the Academy are overwhelmingly white and old and any screening is preceded by much huffing and puffing as they and their spouses blow up the anti-hemorrhoid cushions they carry. Maybe they should jazz up their weird monument to a dying industry by having the starchitect responsible for the eyesore plastering R.I.P. across it.

*

On the other hand, the movies have been dying since they were born. Many lamented the demise of the silent era because for the first time there had been a global dramatic language apart from the ballet, a visual one that they hoped would bring universal understanding.

The Talkies might not have made it had not the almost coincident invention of air conditioning made movie-going through the Thirties less of a sweat soaked ordeal in much of the States. Television threatened the business in the Fifties and then spawned the VCR and CD which gave it a new revenue stream.

Some time ago I visited my features agent in the United Talent Agency offices in Beverly Hills where all you could hear was the chirping of crickets and snores of the assistants whose phones hadn't rung for days.

He admitted the industry was reeling with the impact of the internet and there were those who were afraid it was going to go down the tubes, as the music business had done. He however was sure that within eighteen months they would have figured out how to monetize the Web and sure enough Netflix and other streaming services revealed another pot of gold. He was right. Yet again a technological innovation had come to the rescue.

In the early Fifties Selznick mused that *Hollywood's like Egypt. Full of crumbled pyramids. It'll just keep crumbling until finally the wind blows the last studio prop against the sands.* Getting on for seventy years later the pyramids are still standing.

*

Producers will be an important part of your working life and your relationship with them will be crucial. It's important to understand what drives them and how that differs from what drives you.

In a very hip store in Santa Monica I witnessed an incident that demonstrated the producer gene at work outside the studio, involving someone I shall also have to call X. He and his brother were and remain successful and scarily litigious producers.

While I was having a discreet look at the price label while pretending to feel the weight of the material, I saw there was a commotion at the cash register. Edging towards it after recognizing him, I saw that he and his entourage were engaged in dispute with the polite but harassed sales clerk.

The point of contention was a dozen Nate Naste silk shirts, then quite the thing for the portly man because the virulence of their patterns disguised the effects of too many good lunches and dinners. (An alternative title to this book would be *With Knife and Fork through Hollywood – Thirty Years and Never Paid for Lunch.*)

The producer was insisting that the store's own wooden hangers be included with the sale. The clerk said that wouldn't be possible but he would provide hangers just as good – even better in fact. The producer's counter was that he would walk away from the entire deal and leave the shirts on the rack rather than go without the hangers.

He liked the shirts. He really liked the shirts. His credit card was in his hand – see? – ready to part with fifteen hundred dollars. But no way was he going to pass the card over unless the hangers — worth probably ten bucks in total — were thrown in.

It ended with his getting the shirts and the hangers and I realized, as I continued not shopping, that I had just seen what, on the one hand, was irrational, self-destructive behavior but which was also the height of rationality if you were a producer.

As a writer you'll sweat and fret every word and every punctuation mark, trying to balance sense with rhythm and couching it in terms of how that character would speak. For X, the equivalent was negotiating every single point of even the most minor deal so that not one half cent would be left on the table.

I have another tell-tale sighting of this same producer at a screening. The British director of the movie had promised to deal with all the notes he'd been given but didn't change a thing. If anything he'd doubled down on what X didn't want.

When that dawned on X he jumped up from his seat, marched down the aisle, pushed past the members of the public in the director's row of seats, grabbed him by the throat and started choking him. Perhaps it was just as well for the hapless sales clerk that he blinked over the hangers.

*

The producing gene is as rare as the gene for anything truly extraordinary and I've often thought it akin to a musician having perfect pitch.

If there's a whiff of the scoundrel about some of them when that money runs short it's possible to forgive them because of what they create. In Sam Spiegel's case, *Suddenly Last Summer*, *The African Queen*, *On the Waterfront*, *The Bridge over the River Kwai* and *Lawrence of Arabia*, among others.

On his uppers in London at one low point he phoned a London lawyer at random. Talking quickly he explained that the lawyer didn't know him but he needed five thousand pounds to pay his hotel bill. Would this total stranger give him a loan?

The lawyer hung up but was intrigued. Telling his wife that he was about to do the stupidest thing in his life, he called by the expatriate American's hotel. Sure enough, his caller was holed up in his room, afraid even to leave it in case his luggage was impounded by the management.

Impressed by Spiegel's *chutzpah* the lawyer wrote the check and expected never to see a penny of it or the recipient again. When he came into funds the first thing Spiegel did was repay the money with interest and send a ton of business the lawyer's way for the rest of his career.

One of the ways he obtained those funds was by some typical quick thinking. Observing that one of the private dining rooms in the very expensive hotel was being prepared for a party, he slipped inside. Reading the name tags he realized the event would be in honor of the most important British film producer of the day. It was the work of a moment to abstract one of the cards, write his own name on it and place it next to that of the guest of honor.

The eminent Brit was at first puzzled by this unknown American on his immediate right; then charmed and finally bowled over. When Spiegel carefully let slip that he was on the point of securing the rights to a current best seller the producer hurriedly proposed a deal. Why didn't they split the acquisition cost and co-produce the movie?

Spiegel agreed. Once the check was in his pocket he used it to raise an equivalent sum and buy out the person who actually did own the rights.

*

The one thing that all successful producers have in common is an attention to detail. Selznick's collected memos show an almost pathological need to get them right – even to the shape of the ice cubes in a mint julep in Civil War Atlanta. He also had a life-long fascination for English tailoring and shoe-making, themselves accretions of detail.

Once your disbelief is suspended by even the smallest detail you realize that what you're watching is only a bunch of actors standing in front of painted canvas.

Sometimes that attention to detail can be pushed to the very edge of the envelope. On one production the studio head, on visiting the set, was puzzled to note that almost every male actor seemed to be of varying acting ability but all of the same height.

The costume of the two actors who were noticeably shorter and taller seemed not to fit them, being too short in the leg or else with the pants pinned up. The taller one was wearing excellent shoes but limping because they were at least a size too small for him. Despite the summer theme of the script, every actor's wardrobe list contained a Burberry's raincoat and hat from Bates of St. James, London.

On looking at the script he noticed that many of the names had been changed and that the substitute names all had the same initials. Mystery deepened when he saw the huge pile of hand-made luggage, wallets, passport covers and briefcases, most of it also from fashionable and expensive Jermyn Street, which had been delivered to the set.

A great deal of the budget seemed to have been spent on ordering luxury items which would rate only a passing glance from the camera at most. All of them had those initials embossed, usually in gold.

The penny dropped when he realized those initials were those of the producer who was hedging his bets against a box office flop by intending to carry off on the last day of production several tens of thousands of dollars-worth of handmade English shoes, leather items, suits, jackets, shirts, overcoats, cuff links, wallets, cigarette cases, cigar cutters and tie pins, each of them in his size and, where possible, with his initials engraved on them.

Mischief? Creativity? Borderline malfeasance? Outright theft? It's sometimes hard to draw the line but I can't resist a sneaking admiration for those who live by their wits.

*

Having suggested what your relationship should be with directors and producers – professional, punctual, alert and polite unless boundaries are crossed – I should add a note about actors. The problem is I'm not sure if they actually exist. If they do they obey the laws of the quantum world and not ours.

An elemental particle cannot be said with any certainty to be in any one place at any one time. The act of observing it with, say, a proton bumps it out of position. All you can do is guess where it might be. It's the same with actors.

On one level Los Angeles is full of them. There are even more of them than there are screen-writers and bail bondsmen. They wait tables, valet cars, take Pilates and head off to their yoga sessions with those little mats rolled up under their arms. Those who claim to have spoken to them report that their conversation is full of auditions, job offers and acting classes. They also seem to complain a lot about not being offered work.

Try to book one, however, for a single day's shoot or an entire movie and they disappear. They're waiting a call-back on a pilot they read for. Or they've gone to New York for a stage play. Or they don't want to go on location because they're in the middle of a divorce. Or they've read the sides their agent sent them and this character isn't for them.

It's confounding but all too true. When you don't need them, they're all over the place. When you do, they vanish.

11

PRACTICAL ECSTASY

It was only when I heard the whine of the siren behind me that I looked down at the dashboard. Oooops. I was doing one hundred and twenty miles an hour and even in Arizona that's frowned upon. The Colt Single Action Army Pistol is the official state firearm of The Apache State and the fact that it even has one tells you something about it.

Courteous Vigilance is the motto of the Department of Public Safety whose officer was on my tail. They had recently been in the news when one of his colleagues pointed a gun at a seven-year-old child in a traffic stop while threatening to shoot the driver. That incident was caused by a mistake in the stolen vehicle registry but in my case I was unnegotiably fifty-five miles an hour over the speed limit.

What saved me were the vestigial traces of my Irish accent, overlaid as it is by decades in the States. I'd lucked into being stopped by a cop with Irish ancestry.

Americans really do like the Irish and it's a card to play in situations like this. If I'd pulled out a fiddle and danced a jig for him in a green kilt he couldn't have been happier so he wrote the ticket down to ninety-six miles an hour and spared me losing my car and spending time in the lock-up and I kept my foot off the gas for the rest of the trip.

I was doing a swing through the desert states of Arizona, Nevada and the sandier bits of California. Deserts certainly put you in your place and I always find them unnerving and compulsively interesting. They don't give a damn for us, never noticed our arrival and won't remember us when we've gone. In many ways like show business itself.

The baking rock of the bluffs looks like frozen noise from some great convulsion in a prehistoric past that is still, out there, the present. Some years ago the words *alluvial fan* stuck in my mind and the narrow road runs past those vast piles of rubble which sweep down from the mountains.

I was taking the slow way to Death Valley to find a tunnel which had been dug by a miner over the course of forty years of single handed toil. Neither you nor I have any clue what bauxite is or what they do with it but there are people obsessed with the stuff, whatever it is.

He'd arrived as a young man, realized that carting it away for those who mined it was the way to riches but had been stymied by a mountain which blocked the way to market. Rolling up his sleeves, he'd attacked the rock face and had still been at it, forty years later, when his heart gave out with the tunnel cut only half way through.

Ten years or so after he'd commenced he'd had only several hundred yards completed when the mines closed and the miners moved on. There was no point – if there ever had been – to his tunnel. There never would be any need for it. Ten years of back breaking labor in hundred-degree heat were, as far as the rest of the world was concerned, wasted.

Refusing to brood or second guess his original ambition he kept on working. Day after day for the thirty years which comprised the rest of his life, he kept up his dynamiting, pickaxe and shovel wielding and endless effort of pushing the spoil out to the tunnel mouth.

I never got to what the local guides refer to as a folly. A flash flood had washed out any passable road to it. I'd thought there might be a story with a blackly comic edge to it but instead I found a way of thinking about the day-to-day writing life. You'll be in a kind of tunnel there, too.

Now and again you'll manage to drive it through the mountain and see the project all the way through to the screen. Sometimes – maybe more often than not – it will never see the light of day. You can't regard the time and effort spent on it as wasted. Writers write. That's what they do.

Some movies get made and some plays get put on. Others remain on the shelf. Whatever happens, your job is to heft that case of dynamite and your pickaxe and spade to where you left off the day before. Some days you'll measure progress in inches. Others, you'll cover page after page. It's what you signed up for.

*

Flann O'Brien uses the same metaphor in *A Bash In The Tunnel,* his essay on James Joyce. In it he tells the tale of a Dubliner who found himself locked in a train carriage one Friday night. Not required for service until Monday, the carriage was shunted about all weekend, across the marshaling yards.

By good fortune the carriage contained the bar and it was the work of a moment for the captive to force it open. Manfully he then set to work to demolish the contents one by one, through the night and the next day. Ignoring the squealing of the wheels and sudden bumps and reversings, he applied himself to the task of clearing shelf after shelf of whisky, gin, brandy and sherry with frequent refreshings of lighter fare such as beer and wine.

A heroic task! By Monday morning the bar had been cleared and he'd not noticed the dozens of miles he and the carriage had covered.

O'Brien offers us a Joyce equally drunk on words and their possibilities, working his way along the bar in *Finnegan's Wake*, heedless of the world outside and its convulsions. All that mattered was draining the glass or the bottle in front of him. Each working day was one to look forward to.

It would be at the same time identical to the day before it and yet totally fresh. On waking there would be a sense of anticipation of the task ahead, the page or chapter or scene to be achieved. That sense of anticipation would be a physical as well as mental one, a tingling feeling in the hands and gut. That may be why it's so addictive.

Oliver Sacks talked about part of his addiction to writing being the fact that hours would pass without his being aware of the outside world and yet, at their close, he would have achieved something concrete in the pages he'd produced.

*

God forbid I should suggest writing as therapy – especially given the neuroses, twitches and brain staggers that so many of my colleagues seem to suffer from – but there's no doubt that a kind of practical ecstasy is inseparable from the act of writing.

Lawrence Kasdan reports research which indicates that every ninety minutes our brains reset themselves; there's a mental clock which refreshes the mental mechanism for another ninety minutes of effort. If that's so, it's confirmation of Anthony Trollope's dictum that you should write for no more than three hours – two periods of ninety minutes – on any one project.

Such hours are the stuff of a writing life. It's great if the project gets made – if the tunnel gets completed and the bauxite business booms – but not everything you write is going to end up on stage or on screen. Given that, you might as well enjoy the time you're going to spend at the rock face and regard the things which do get made as a bonus.

*

Now and again you might feel that you need somebody alongside you in the tunnel, to share some of the burden or strike sparks off. There have been some legendarily successful writing partnerships and sometimes that Hegelian dialectical of thesis-antithesis-synthesis, is facilitated when you have somebody else in the room. At its best such a partnership can be a kind of marriage. At its worst it can also be a kind of marriage.

Many tag team writers can't envisage writing any other way, despite the fact that you have to split the money. The strongest partnerships manage to survive the fact that the other writer is bringing not just themselves but their spouse, kids, grandparents and out of work, annoying jerk of a brother-in-law into the room; the whole gallery of those the end result has to support financially.

If you can find your other, possibly better, writing half and handle the practical consequences, go for it. At the very least it means there's somebody to blame when it all goes wrong. It may have been that consideration which led me on my own Lonely Hearts quest to find somebody to work with.

*

The collaborator I had in mind was, moment by moment, the funniest human being I'd ever met. He'd moved to LA on the strength of one stage play that indicated he could write fast, snappy dialogue. Very much the kind of dialogue that sitcoms need.

If you're a writer on one of those shows that's successful enough to go into syndication your daily beauty regimen will be having the housekeeper rub you down with hundred dollar bills. Problem was that this particular potential sidekick wanted to be a heavyweight dramatist in the mold of O'Neill or Albee.

This is a guy who could wander into the kitchen of a busy Chinese restaurant and five minutes later the staff would be holding their sides, roaring with laughter, even though neither he nor they spoke each other's language. Something happened when he sat down to write, however. The gags came easily – maybe too easily – but he was impatient with form and structure.

Something even worse happened when he went to pitch meetings. Instead of being the funniest guy in the room he pulled on the mantle of gloomy genius, prickly and argumentative. On one pitch that was otherwise going well he cratered the whole deal by saying he'd expect enough money from it to buy a plane. The executives on the other side of the table thought he was joking but he meant it.

Crazy stuff and he paid the price. By the time I began wooing him he'd been eighteen years in Hollywood and, in his own words, spent them driving in circles around studio parking lots getting nowhere. A good line. A great line. You see why I wanted to have a partnership in which I'd come up with the story outline and structure while he knocked out the zingers and did some character riffs that would lead to riches.

He was agreeable because I had the career he thought he was due and we met every Tuesday night for three or four months to bash things out. I even brought to the table a potential deal at HBO, based on a foreign language movie so this wasn't just that tasty aerial treat, pie in the sky.

*

I had a great time at these dinners, don't get me wrong. I've never laughed so hard since the goat attacked my uncle in the shower. My potential writing partner was, in many ways, at his best. The gags, impressions, juggling with knives and forks, regaling the wait staff and other diners with a stream of improv better than anything at the Saturday night show at The Groundlings couldn't be beat.

It was also him at his worst because any attempt to move on to hammering out a way forward on the script idea in front of us led to a state of despondency, then rage and vituperation against the system and those who worked in it.

There really isn't too much original that can be said in that department. Disappointed writers have been saying it ever since the industry took root in the desert sands and guess what – nobody begged us to come out here or promised that there was a gig for us. I have yet to see the posters that read Two Thousand Screenwriters Wanted! No Experience Necessary! Apply At Once!

It was possible to bend the bow of his anger towards a more comical expression of his grievances but when I suggested he could use this as a basis for a one-man show, he really lost it.

He'd come to Los Angeles to write hefty, enduring works that would take their place in the canon of serious American writing, not turn himself into a raree show or carnival act.

The Big Avocado might have been exactly the wrong place to favor that ambition. It's a place where you can arrive full of dreams and wake up fifty years later with a great tan and not much else to show for it. My counter argument was that Los Angeles was, at heart, a collection of raree shows and carnival acts and why not mine from his experiences a show that would (1) make money and (2) allow him to vent his spleen.

Vain argument. Wasted jaw flap. It was going to be the Great American Novel in movie form or nothing. And we know how that ends. The Mohave, of which Los Angeles is the most extreme extension, the place where it meets the Pacific, is littered with the bones of Great American Writers.

Our Tuesday evenings petered out and a couple of years later I heard he had accepted what he would see as defeat and gone back to where he began, to resume an advertising career. Nothing wrong with that, of course. Isn't Salman Rushdie credited with the cream-cake slogan 'Naughty but nice'?

Much as I believe that the Gods of Comedy rule, especially in my business, I can spot a Tragedy when it's in front of me. The root of it, in this case, lay in not accepting where the grain of genius lay.

Simon Callow once said that you need a talent for having a talent and one of the worst offenses against whatever Gods there are is willfully turning your back on the one you've been given. If the good angels leave one gift in your cradle, you're lucky. To root around sulkily for another or toss away the one you have is an existential affront to them, of which no good will come.

*

The search for a collaborator paid off handsomely for an imaginary writer friend of mine, however. Down on his luck, about to lose his house and car, he woke up one night to hear somebody tapping on his laptop. It was an elf who had heard about the trouble he was in and offered to help out by writing a movie for him.

By dawn he'd finished it and by close of business that day it had been sold. It got made, had a hundred-million-dollar opening weekend and got him a three-picture-deal at a major studio. The elf wrote all three and each was a bigger hit than the previous.

The writer was by now living in a fifty-million-dollar beach house in Malibu, married to the hottest actress in Hollywood and had bought a private jet. When he signed the deal for his next movie the elf said shyly that he had a request. This time could he get at least part of the screenplay credit?

Share my credit? screamed my friend. *Get the fuck out of here.*

*

There are hazards to working with someone and putting your career into their hands. Take the sad story of Chilly and Willy. Not their real names but people I might work with again. Hollywood is a small town and you learn not to give offense unless you mean to. Everybody tends to eat in the same places and talk about the same things so over the years you keep your voice down and sometimes, to an outsider, talk in what seem to be circles.

The waitress or waiter slinging your butterflied lamb chop down on the table is probably an actor eager to pick up and retain any overheard gossip and you never know when a careless word will bite you in the ass. For some years I had a Pilates instructor who was more clued into who was in and who was out in the studios than the ace reporters of Variety because of what he was told while working out his clients.

For some years Chilly and Willy had been knocking on the door as producers. They were a big enough deal to have an office but not so big that it was on the lot. They picked up their own overhead – which usually means a bored and attractive girl sulkily buffing her nails and refusing to answer the phone – and could get a meeting but to date that had been it.

I forget what project they hooked into that looked set to change the mold but their pitch went over big. So big they got an offer in the room. If you pulled something like that off, you would be pointed out by quavering old-timers decades later in the retirement home as somebody who sold the sucker *in the room*.

They were on the verge of selling their movie to one of the major studios, which would have made them players overnight. Just before the handshake to seal the deal Chilly turned to Willy and said he'd like to have a word in private.

A puzzled Willy followed him to the corridor and asked *what the fuck?* A look of low cunning crossed Chilly's face as he said they should say they wanted to think about the terms of the deal overnight. That would show they weren't pikers who needed to rush into something.

Willy pointed out with some heat that they *were* pikers and they *did* need to rush into something. Such as getting back into the room forthwith and asking for the lawyers to draw the paperwork up and the studio cashier the check. *We have the fish on the hook,* was Chilly's reply. *We don't have to rush this.*

They could take twenty-four hours, get the deal improved by a couple of zeros and percentage points and maybe finagle some perks for themselves, like first class air travel to the location for family members. *Don't sweat it* he said and Willy ultimately agreed.

They went back into the room with a quiet swagger and said they appreciated the offer but would like a day to think it over, letting the suggestion hang in the air that they had every other studio in town in their back pocket.

*

I don't know if Chilly and Willy stopped off to window-shop at the Ferrari dealership on the way back home but it's likely they split a bottle of champagne with their respective partners that night and the celebratory action in the sack was tumultuous. Around four that morning they would have felt the bedroom shake not because of further sexual activity but because the LA basin was being rocked by a pretty severe earthquake.

LA closed down for several days after that trembler which came in at something over six point five, which is when you really take notice. When the shaking stopped and the studio opened up again the following week there was a backlog of business to attend to.

When they finally got through to the executive who wanted their movie so badly she said Nah, she'd been thinking it over and it didn't really fit in with the studio's plans for the next production cycle after all. No doubt they'd set it up with whoever else had been interested.

She wished them luck and that was that. They never made the movie and Chilly and Willy didn't remain partners much longer. They had pissed on their own peaches.

*

Pissing on your own peaches is a technical term derived from the story of two producers who are the only survivors of a plane crash in the Sahara. After stumbling over miles of sand dunes in one hundred and fifty degree heat they see something glinting in the sand.

Digging it up they find that it's a can of peaches in golden syrup. Even more miraculously it's ice cold. Things get even better when they discover a can opener and two spoons. Opening it they see it's filled with glistening, ripe, cold, juicy peaches.

As the first producer gets ready to dig his spoon into them the second says *Wait. Let's piss on them first.*

12

NOT WAITING FOR THE PHONE TO RING

Writing for hire shouldn't mean just waiting for the phone to ring. Sometimes you're going to be so inspired by a story that you'll write it on spec or try to find someone to pay you for the script. Where do you find those stories?

Real life offers a continual supply of goodies, often based on just how nuts ordinary folk can be –

> *Item: Kelli Peters was the subject of an anonymous phone call to the authorities. A man said one of the volunteers at the school in Irvine, California was driving 'very erratically' and seemed to be under the influence of drugs. Police came and, in front of other parents and children at the school searched Kelli's car, where they found a bag of marijuana, a ceramic pot pipe and pills. Kelli insisted the drugs weren't hers.*

> *Two other parents, then-married couple Kent and Jill Easter, both practicing attorneys, were later found to have planted them inside her car – the apex of a yearlong campaign of retaliation against Kelli. The couple's conflict with Kelli appears to have begun in February 2010, when Jill came to pick up her son from school and found that he wasn't waiting for her.*

> *Kelli told her the boy had been 'a little slow' – meaning he hadn't joined the lineup at the same time as the other students. Jill took it as a derogatory comment regarding her son's intelligence. Jill and her then-husband Kent tried to get Kelly fired, an attempt that culminated with planting drugs in her car.*

You wouldn't make it up and thankfully you don't have to. One of my oldest friends in Hollywood, Jeff Wachtel from Universal started out scouring the media for crime and disaster stories like this. Every time identical twins fell down a disused mineshaft in Appalachia, he was on the next plane out to secure their life rights.

I've also covered a fair bit of North America on similar missions. That's how I picked up most of what there is to know about the professional wrestling circuit while researching the death of a wrestler in the ring; how I came to drive a NASCAR motorized coffin around the track at one hundred and eighty terrifying miles an hour; why I spent a couple of weeks with a guy who sold the US Defense Department on his psychic powers; another job took me to Virginia with the people who run the organ transplant registry and train those whose job it is to ask the grieving to consider giving up their loved one's organs at point of death; I spent an equally sobering week visiting murder scenes in Flatbush in the company of an expert in the Jewish Mob and an even more sobering one on San Quentin's Death Row on another gig.

There were also some moments of absolute privilege, such as spending two weeks at the Harlem Dance Theatre with its founder Arthur Mitchell. The time spent at Josephine Baker's chateau in the company of one of her Rainbow Children was also magical.

*

I always caution the person I'm negotiating with that when you sell the rights to Hollywood, one of the rights you're selling is the right to get indignant with what we'll do with it. Usually they go ahead anyway, such is the lure of having their story told on the screen.

Sometimes you need to be careful, too, even with the resources of a studio behind you. The Austrian Felix Salten picked up a hefty check from Walt Disney when Walt bought the rights to his 1923 novel *Eine Lebensgeschichte aus dem Walde* which was given the snappier title of *Bambi*.

The generations who were charmed by the adventures of the nipple-less deer might not have cared to know that Salten was the leading pornographer of his day. His novel *Josefine Mutzenbacher: Die Lebensgeschichte einer Wienerischen Dirne. Von ihr selbst erzählt (The Diary of a Viennese Whore As Told By Herself)* was not, as far as I can establish, picked up by Disney Animation and isn't coming to a theatre near you any time soon.

I suggest not falling asleep while telling the story as one Academy Award nominated director and writer did during his own pitch meeting. There was a long pause during which everyone assumed he was thinking hard with his chin on his chest about how to explain the next narrative development of his own idea. The pause went on and his breathing became undeniably a snore. That project didn't sell.

Nor did one during which I suffered an even greater loss of mental motive power. Normally I enjoy pitching, one of the last vestiges of the immemorial tradition of oral story-telling. This time I was late for the meeting and only learned on the way in that it had been set up as a favor to the director.

The prospective producer's lack of response to my opening paragraphs suggested he modeled for one of the Easter Island statues. It's much easier to pitch to somebody who responds to what they're hearing, even if it's to lean over the waste basket and throw up.

Five minutes in I had what I can only describe as an out of body experience, floating eerily above the conference room table, listening to my own voice coming from what seemed to be a mile-long hollow metal tube.

Another part of me was thinking what a waste of everybody's time this was and then the voice stopped. In the silence it occurred to me that I really should get on to the next story point but when I went to the Cupboard of Memory, it was bare.

Ever had your car lose all its electrics in the middle of the fast lane? The lights in the dashboard of my brain went out, the engine died and all that could be heard was the quiet whisper of the air conditioning going through one of my ears and out of the other one, meeting no resistance on the way.

After a couple of weeks that was actually only thirty seconds or so the frantic prompts of the director tried to bring me round but this was total and complete collapse of the brain matter. Oddly peaceful, in a way.

Perhaps I had quite unexpectedly achieved Nirvana and been released from suffering, desire, the sense of self, the effects of karma and the cycle of death and rebirth. More likely my conscious brain had parted company with my unconscious due to complete lack of interest in the material.

At times like these those with presence of mind fake epileptic fits. All I did was mutter something about having had to deal with some fairly major family issues recently and suggest we meet some other time.

Needless to say we didn't and I never worked with or for that director again. That experience taught me not to take the machinery in the skull lightly. If pushed too hard it would rebel.

*

Edgar Wallace employed three short-hand typists to whom he dictated the day's output; while the previous was typing the stuff up he dictated to the next, off the top of his head.

The hyper-prolific Wallace needed an industrial work ethic. At one point his publishers claimed that one quarter of all books currently in publication were written by him. He too was lured to Hollywood, working as script supervisor for RKO. Among other projects, he outlined the first notes on what would become *King Kong*.

One Friday evening he suddenly remembered that he was contract bound to deliver a full-length thriller by Monday morning. Hiring a team of typists, he dictated through that night, all day Saturday, through Sunday and Sunday night and sent the completed manuscript off first thing next day. Then he promptly experienced a complete nervous collapse and had to be hospitalized.

At times, under the press of deadline and bank balance I've had to write on more than one project in a day. I've found it possible to write on three separate ones, helped by strict adherence to the rule never to spend more than three hours on any one idea.

Four is a bridge too far and I caution against it. It really does lead to bits flying off the brain, eyestrain, and hearing voices. Even Isaac Newton, after all, said that it was only possible for him to follow an uninterrupted train of thought to its conclusion for forty-five seconds at a time. He'd noticed, however, that most of his fellow men could do so for only five or ten consecutive seconds.

That sounds preposterous but try it and you'll be humbled. Our chain of thought about plot, character development and exposition of theme is made of very short links. We need to have respect for the mental mechanism which processes them. Just as an athlete's performance has an upper limit, so does that of those who mine their imaginations for a living.

Mental fatigue is insidious because it means we lose focus on the need to get the exact word in the right place. In an art gallery in Vienna I read the manifesto of the Austrian surrealist Konrad Klapheck alongside one of his paintings –

> My main weapons are humor and precision.
> Only the coldness of precision gives you access
> to the celebrations of the soul.

That icy, lofty precision is what we're looking for every second of our working lives as we explore our own souls and try to communicate with those of others.

*

It can be demoralizing to take your dog and pony show on the road time after time and not make a sale. Fortunately I had my stage career running in tandem with my screen career. This meant there was always a project on my desk. The more you write, in any medium, the more you learn about writing.

Alongside the screen work I did all over the world, I found time for the demands of the stage; enduring the drafty rehearsal space, the weak tea and instant coffee and, if in the UK, the crunch of biscuit crumbs underfoot (why are British actors so obsessed with custard creams?) and the usually derisory financial rewards.

When I worked briefly in the Unemployment Benefits Office, a cunning Liverpudlian caused enormous bureaucratic headaches by claiming his profession to be that of Coronation Day Flag Seller. The regularity of his employment was probably greater than that of most in theatre and yet we persevere.

In a letter to the perpetually complaining Arnold Wesker, Robert Bolt, playwright and screenwriter, talked of how we are lucky if even one tongue of the flame from the volcano churning inside the writer gets communicated to the audience. When you feel that you might be able to do that in front of a live audience, even once, you're hooked. For life.

I'm not totally sure, however, that movie or TV executives share the same enthusiasm. In fact when it comes to Hollywood I'd recommend being circumspect about your theatre work.

It's probably safer never to even admit that you've been to a stage show. Or know about them. You can claim to have vaguely heard of Broadway or the West End but only in connection with a movie or TV star acting in that quaint old-fashioned thing

A Play For The Stage

This isn't because you're dealing with morons. There are technical issues here, connected with a plausible fear that someone who has written stage plays won't understand the more plastic language of the camera; that they'll be unable to handle more characters than two and more locations than one.

Not all stage writers can manage the transition to the screen or wish to try. It's a different medium with different rules, mostly involving Point of View. Used to directing the audience's attention with words or, at best, a stage picture, it can be hard to let go of that and allow the camera to do the work.

The death of the three-act play has resulted in playwrights having to cram all they have to say into two acts or, increasingly, one – although George Bernard Shaw did say that any damn fool could write the first act of a play. The received wisdom in the world of the linear movie narrative is that you need three acts to tell a fully rounded story.

I suspect there is also a suspicion that play writers, in their hearts, look down their noses at the brash but terminally insecure executives they're dealing with, while taking the moolah. The financial rewards of writing solely for the stage are of course astronomical, in the sense that you usually need a telescope to see them.

*

In the early days of motion pictures the words on the cards were often written by female studio employees and for many years they were as likely to be the scenarists of the silent movies as men. Then the talkies came in and Hollywood panicked, realizing that they would now need a pipeline of words as well as images.

Where to get them? The obvious place was Broadway and for many years the Twentieth Century Limited carried boxcars of playwrights West, to be put to work in the lucrative salt mines of the Writer's Bungalows. Among them were William Faulkner and Clifford Odets.

Soon, however, it was clear that many of those writers had no talent for or wish to learn the rules of writing for the camera or, even worse, had left wing sympathies. The movies, in the moguls' eyes, were a place of refuge from the Depression, not the place to probe the reasons for it.

Off they went, back to their novels and Little Theaters and dreams of inciting the working class to outrage in New York, a safe two and a half thousand miles away from the industry which owned the most powerful tool of mass indoctrination ever invented.

*

In their place arose generations of writers who not only understood the rules of motion picture dramatic construction but the rules of surviving in what was pretty much a factory system.

Money and talent went in one end and out came the finished, mass produced product. It was a good deal all around if somewhat limiting as to how much the movie industry could question the political, economic and cultural system it operated so successfully in.

This was a period during which the studios each turned out thirty to forty movies a year on average with the same ruthless efficiency that Detroit turned out automobiles. Every afternoon the number of feet of film shot and number of scenes in the can had to be reported upwards.

If it fell below what was expected of a director on Irving Thalberg's lot, his driver was sent to stand on the sound stage in the director's eyeline; a not so subtle hint that if he didn't bring in his numbers he'd be sent home early and put on suspension. Too many suspensions and he'd have to hand in the megaphone and get a proper job.

*

The most useful note I can give you about pitch and script meetings, especially ones on a project not yet green-lit, is to explain what the phrase that ends so many of them actually means.

The phrase is

We are really going to make this movie.

And it means

This movie is never going to get made and you'll never hear from us again.

It's not a manipulation. They're not lying when they tell you the project is about to go. They really do want to make your movie *while you are in the room with them* but this meeting has been one of a half dozen they'll take today. On your way in to it you passed the previous hopefuls exiting and when you leave you'll pass the next group heading in.

The average short-term specific memory span of mammals is twenty-seven seconds. Even your dog that you think is so smart forgets everything after two minutes and has to start again. It's the same with the people you just met. To compensate they have what your dog also has, a conditioned set of responses to danger which helps them stay alive.

The dog almost instantly forgets what you just told it about peeing on the couch. The executives even more instantly forget how great your movie sounded. The dog does, however, retain the information that jumping into the open fire is a bad idea.

The executive knows that the greatest danger to his or her career is okaying something that turns out to be a stinker. That's the equivalent of jumping into the fire. Far better not to green-light anything at all.

Ever.

13

TAKE THE GIG

I t's seldom that your career path will be impacted by a disruption in the earth's crust but Chilly and Willy's misadventures pose another question – to what extent should you try to strategize your career as opposed to taking every job that comes along. Mike Tyson avers that no plan for a boxing match survives the first punch on the nose so why try to plot out your moves in such a volatile business as entertainment?

I recently passed the four-million-mile mark on my frequent flier account because my inclination has always been to

TAKE THE GIG

Someone asked Haydn why he hadn't written more string quartets and he said it was because nobody asked him to. Provided the money's on the table and I feel emotionally or intellectually connected to the project, I'm inclined to say Yes. Now and again, of course, it's a wobbler. You're being asked to take it on trust that this project is the goods and has a chance of getting made.

*

If the bank balance is dwindling and you start to think that cat food is so expensive it must be fit for human consumption, you might be tempted to swallow your doubts and take on a stinker. In my early days in Hollywood I got called to a meeting on a project provisionally entitled *Doctor Plastic,* with the logline *Plastic Surgeon by Day – Crime Fighter by Night.*

The hook was that after his wife was murdered, LA's most prominent cosmetic surgeon built a machine to constantly change his features so that he could bring criminals to book, without discovery.

Okay, you're pulling a face but intergenerational wealth has been created from ideas like that. I'd almost persuaded myself that something could be done with it when a minor point occurred to me. I asked wouldn't that mean that you'd need a different actor every week to play the hero?

I was sure they'd thought of that and how to keep the viewer from being confused about whose story they were following. That was only a technical issue, of course and no doubt they already had the answer.

A long silence followed. A very long silence. They hadn't thought of it. That project died and with it the temptation I'd nearly given into, to sell out even before I'd gotten established.

You have to be careful. A writer friend of mine, in a lean spell, took up the offer of a Bollywood producer to fly to Mumbai on an all-cash deal. Not only would he not have to share any of the loot with the tax authorities, the Writers Guild of America (West) wouldn't take its share towards pension and benefits.

On arrival he was installed in something much less than a five-star hotel, his passport was confiscated – he never did see it again – and he was handed a pile of video cassettes of current Hollywood movies. His job was to copy them word for word so that pirate versions of them could be made on a shoestring for the vast subcontinental distribution network.

When he protested at the potential legal consequences he was told the cunning plan. Now and again he would *dialogue in* – their exact phrase – a couple of lines of his own. This, he was assured, was a fool-proof way to stay out of the courts.

With no passport, dead broke and relying on them to send a couple of meals a day to his room, he set to work. An unusually virulent strain of amoebic dysentery laid him low and when I saw him again, months after his escape, he had shed a score of pounds. If they made even a percentage of the scripts he had banged out for them he would be in the record books as a writer even more prolific than Edgar Wallace.

Another way to get a toe-hold in the industry is through reality TV. A friend of mine became script writer on a reality show while waiting for his big break. You didn't know they had them? You thought unscripted television was unscripted?

After working on a number of shows he walked away when they attached him to a game show on basic cable that would be set in a men's restroom. While at the stall or trough the player would be surprised by the compere, with an invitation to answer general knowledge questions for cash. The working title was *Urine The Money*.

My own adventures and misadventures in Tinsel Town never took me to reality TV but I had one dalliance with the advertising industry. This was in connection with the first TV commercial for Elizabeth Taylor's *White Diamond* line of fragrances.

Come with me into the whacky world of a superstar who had been persuaded to give her imprimatur to a perfume. The thirty second television commercial announcing this stupendous event was treated by its makers as if it was a major motion picture and its budget, kept under wraps, astronomical.

By the time I got horn-swaggled into this project I was accustomed to the vast number of people involved in a shoot – the studio flacks, the network flacks, the production company flacks. In this new world I discovered even more layers of those charged with obstructing progress – in this case the advertising agency flacks and those from 'The Client', which was a word whispered by the Armani-clad execs much as low ranking employees in the Mob must murmur fearfully about the *capo du tutti capo*.

The Client, the perfume company arm of the cosmetics firm behind the folly, had been persuaded that an Emmy-Winning writer (me) would be an essential part of the team. They didn't want the ad just to be head shots of Liz fondling a tub of the life-changing elixir.

I delivered the goods to order. The idea that ET would play the role of an international diamond smuggler hiding the goods in plain sight excited The Client. The payoff would be when Liz would be confronted by the cops. She'd take the diamonds from her purse and discreetly drop them into the glass of champagne she was drinking. They'd be invisible and she'd be home free.

Not a bad little idea with *Rififi* overtones. In order to pull it off in thirty seconds we'd have to have very tight story telling. The Client, however, wanted a lot of money on the screen so the locations ranged from the *Queen Mary* to a huge mansion in Pasadena with a swimming pool the size of an oil slick and a rain forest set. There was talk of sending Liz and the crew to Hawaii to shoot a real rain forest but even in this feverish world reality sometimes gains a foothold.

*

Trouble started on Day One when the body-double flown in from Nashville ignored her strict instructions to never talk to the star, not even to say Good Morning. Not only did she do that but she said how much she admired her. Inexplicably that was a capital offense in Taylorland and the double was put on a plane back home that afternoon, in tears.

There was a huge series of fights about it which everybody involved seemed to enjoy tremendously. Next day our lead was late on set. Much anxious whispering. It turned out that Ms. Taylor was sulking because no one had given her a little present as a token of their appreciation for her consenting to earn several million of merchandising dollars by putting her heft to sales of the magic toilet water.

That was quickly righted by a visit to Tiffany's on Rodeo Drive and every day thereafter that store or Cartier or Van Cleef and Arpels were put on high alert to come up with something that would cure the sulks.

So the long days wore on until the thing was in the can. I could have hung around the set – I mean this was Elizabeth Taylor – but I prefer my drama on the page and not in real life. It was screened just once, proved conclusively that you can't tell a complete three-act movie in thirty seconds, left the audience in total bewilderment and pulled off the airwaves the very same night.

It was of course replaced by a series of still photos of Elizabeth Taylor, fondling a jar as if it contained a half gallon of the Fountain of Youth.

*

Whatever the writing task is and whatever your approach to it, the bedrock is your own creativity. When we talk about that subject there's a danger of wandering into the Land of the Happy Pink Unicorns, where creativity is an unalloyed, positive and somewhat sappy Good.

As someone who has dealt with his own creative being every day of his working life I can offer some guidance to its darker side; best illustrated by a series of conversations I had with an Irishman who had done serious jail time for paramilitary activities.

He consequently had a wealth of knowledge not just about the terrible years of the Troubles he'd been a player in but insights into the psychology of those involved. Somehow while being hunted by the British Army and trying to keep one step ahead of the killers on the other side, he had time to observe the mechanics of insurgency. Later, in an internment camp, he'd had the enforced leisure to synthesize it.

What he took away from it was that revolutionary action is seldom led by the theorists and strategists. They were good at politics and press relations and the branding of the movement but not so good at actually making things happen on the ground.

The people who really made the difference were the handful of those who just couldn't sit still. In Yiddish this is known as having *shpilkes* – ants in the pants. In Ireland it's known as being a bit of an eejit.

There was always at least one of them in any group of plotters. This was the person whose motives for joining the struggle were less doctrinal than an inability to put their feet up and watch the telly.

Whatever had drawn them to the underground organization, once there they demanded action. If there wasn't a bomb available they lobbied to be allowed to get on the street and ambush an army patrol or kidnap a policeman. If that took too much planning, then how about going out with a handful of bricks and starting a riot? They were the ones who kept the whole thing on the boil and in effect made the blood-spattered history of their times.

In one of the quiet bars where he'd once helped plot murder, he argued that theirs were creative acts. That the act of creation wasn't that Hippy Dipshit New Age Fairy Dust but something often literally explosive.

One constant among the writers and other artists I've known is an echo of an infernal restlessness; a driving energy which is uncomfortable in close up; they always seem to be looking just over your head as if there's something there they need to deal with in a moment, once you're out of the way.

Let's not get too grandiose about this; drinkers have this look in their eyes, too. For them the object of desire is the next bottle or the moment when the bar door is tugged open by Mike the hung-over landlord. It is however living with a purpose outside yourself. If you don't pick up the bomb, glass or pencil, the Armalite, bottle or the paintbrush, nobody will. And it has to be done now, today, this hour, this minute or the moment is going forever.

My guide, however, went on to tell me that he came to feel that the detonation of a bomb made less impact than putting pen to paper. On the surface an explosion or an assassination promised to change things but so often failed. It became one of a series of disjointed events that happened, literally, in a flash and disappeared.

A pen and sheet of paper, on the other hand, were a kind of time machine. If you were looking to dent the curve of history, those were your man and not a bullet or eight ounces of C-4.

Long after you'd gone there would be evidence that X had once marked the spot where you stood and isn't that what we're all engaged in, in the arts? The fretful, unceasing struggle to carve that X as deep in the fabric of time as possible, in the medium that our gifts are best suited for?

14

NEAR-DEATH EXPERIENCE ON WASHINGTON BOULEVARD

That soft spoken but competent and deadly man would have been a good right hand the night Brian Dennehy and I got chased by both the Venice Chapter of the Hells Angels and the Santa Monica Police Department. The events of that fraught night gave me another insight into what my new life on the West Coast would open up to me. It furthered my education in the reality of Los Angeles and how that reality shapes the movies made there.

The evening began in the cafe/bar in Venice – the real Venice, the one in Southern California and not the fake in Italy – owned at that time by Dudley Moore and Tony Bill. At the end of the evening the barman pointed to the twenty-three coffee beans on Brian's saucer which tallied the twenty-three Sambucas he'd manfully disposed of. *You're not driving home tonight, Big Fella*, he told him.

The car keys were handed to me – I was virtually a tee-totaller having only drunk a dozen or so bottles of Guinness – and the valet brought Brian's car to the door. This was a Chevy Caprice which the California Highway Patrol had auctioned off the previous week.

This was a beast of a car which could do one hundred and fifty on the straight, stop on a dime and still had the shotgun racks in the front seat. Keep an eye on those shotgun racks, even though they're empty. They probably saved our lives.

Our way home lay along Washington Boulevard and Brian decided to liven things up by urging me to go faster. Barreling through a red light, I nearly hit a biker wearing the patches of the Venice Chapter, Hell's Angels. He gave us the finger.

Brian naturally climbed into the rear seat, lowered the window and tried to lift the guy off his bike while punching him in the face through his helmet. The biker then flagged down a passing police cruiser which pulled alongside and swung the death ray of its searchlight at us.

It picked out me with the very tight crew cut I had in those days, that made me look like a cross between Robert de Niro's psychopath Travis Bickle in *Taxi Driver* and an escapee from a Russian labor camp. It also picked out Brian, who had just come off a role in *Rambo: Part One* as the bad Sheriff.

It finally picked out the shotgun rack which identified the big ole Chevy as an official law enforcement vehicle and thankfully they put two and two together and came up with five. Assuming, we supposed, that we were undercover cops on a mission, they tooted the horn and drove off.

We relaxed. Then I looked in the rear mirror again. There were now three Hell's Angels following us, with their headlights off and at every intersection more seemed to join them. This did not look good.

Brian was now as sober as he'd been drunk before and I was wondering whether they'd ship my body home to the UK or bury me here. It was at this point that one of us had the bright idea to try to shake them off by driving out to the airport. When in serious trouble like this the last thing you need is a bright idea. Especially if the airport, like LAX, is set in a wasteland of warehouses, factories, storage units and parking lots empty of cars.

An additional suggestion. If you are going to head for a place where an Army Division could be slaughtered to the last man without anyone noticing, take at least a cursory glance at the gas needle first. The one on the big Chevy was hovering on empty by the time we got to the Westchester badlands.

Fortunately we hit on the road to the beach before we ran out of gas or the Angels made their move, dumped the car and split up. It's dark on Venice Beach at that time of night and by keeping in motion until dawn I stayed one step ahead of them.

*

During that long night I resolved not to drink again. Ever. If I was serious about remaining in Los Angeles it was clear that things had to change in that department. I also had time to think about what I had learned about the place I intended to make my new home. The States were epic in a very serious way.

This was not England with palm trees but more like the Ireland where every hedge, hill and back street has at some point mutely witnessed the violence that men do to each other. The Angels no doubt carried guns and I suspect we got away with it because Brian acted so crazily that they must have assumed we were armed to the teeth, too.

The menace never far from American life, especially in Los Angeles, had come very close. It was a menace not only in the people but the landscape itself. In wildfire season clouds of black smoke could be seen from the mountain ranges behind downtown; in wet winters entire hillsides would give way in landslides.

The house that Charles Laughton built in Santa Monica Canyon ended up one hundred feet lower across the Pacific Coast Highway after one storm, around the corner from where we lived. The Rodney King Riots were on the scale of a natural disaster and, living downtown, we were trapped for five days until the fury burned itself out, with the rioters exhausted.

As I – I rack my brains but the only word is 'cowered' – as I cowered on the beach the night I'd come to the realization that LA really was living on the edge, not only of the continent but of human experience. One thing was clear, as the dawn found me, chilled, sore of foot but in one piece and able to limp back to my lodgings.

Things would never be dull here and there were stories to be had. The clear light gave everything a shape and definition and those stories seemed to want to be told very directly.

The Greeks had invented our drama in similar strong, direct light and we were heirs to them, thousands of miles and millennia away. It was all the more astonishing to be living in that light at the Western edge of the Great American Desert having grown up in a part of Ireland so wet that you bought land by the gallon instead of the acre.

*

That Californian light was what bowled over David Hockney when he first went to Los Angeles. His first studio was a mile away from our house and a mutual friend asked if it would be safe for him to visit once the National Guard had secured the streets after the civil disturbances over Rodney King's beating and arrest.

It was a tense time to be driving around that part of Los Angeles, where National Guards units were bivouaced alongside smoldering buildings. Undaunted, Hockey insisted on sketching the ruins of the buildings all around us.

He'd spotted on the TV news the charred air conditioning ducts lying on the ground like entrails. Someone in the car pointed at a particularly dramatic convolution of metalwork and said *Look at that image.* Instantly the painter corrected him. *That's reality,* he said. *The image is what's in your eye.*

The image of Los Angeles that fixed itself in my eye was that of a vast, shapeless city, broiling under an endless angry sun, hemmed in by mountains and the ocean, inhabited by people liable to snap at any time. Dotted here and there were the oddly industrial-looking sound stages of the studios, run by borderline crazy people even more likely to snap at any time.

It would only take one final God Almighty earthquake to lay it open to an Armageddon of wildfires which would drive any survivors into the shark infested waters and the nearest land-fall, unfortunately, is Catalina Island, where they'd stand a good chance of being stomped to death by the buffalo that roam freely across it.

Ireland, according to James Joyce, creates more history than could be consumed locally. Los Angeles seems in its very bones to create more violence, real and fictional, than anywhere else on earth. It's exhilarating and inspirational – assuming you can dodge the flames, the mud-slides, the drive-by shootings, your house being shaken off its foundations and stay one step ahead of the bikers.

*

In the end I gave in, went native and acquired a gun. I might have gone a bit overboard because I bought a .357 Magnum to clear the house of intruders, a semi-automatic Beretta to keep in the glove compartment of the car and a Derringer which could slip into a pocket or garter belt for social occasions; all on the advice of the salesman at Gun Heaven on Pico Boulevard. When I asked for instructions on how to use one he said *Point it, pull the trigger and call the coroner.*

Owning this firepower scared me so much I immediately put them in a gun safe and forgot the combination. Dirty Harry I wasn't.

Guns popped up in show business, too. I went to one script meeting with a producer who gave me a ride back. As he climbed on board I saw there was an ankle holster attached to his leg. When he saw my reaction he proudly pulled out a Glock pistol.

When I asked if he always went to meetings carrying a loaded gun he said *Of course* and when I asked why he replied darkly only that *You never know.*

I don't want to give the impression that Hollywood meetings are always – or often – accompanied by the rattle of gunfire, but that violence just under the surface of American life is extant when you *kill* a deal and *shoot* a scene and hope for your own shows to be a *hit* but the competition's projects to be *dead on arrival* or order somebody to take a *stab* at a rewrite.

I never got so Hollywood rich that I needed a bodyguard as well as the guns but personal protection – not the one in the deodorant commercials – is a constant worry above a certain level of income and fame.

Many recruit their minders from the ranks of Mossad, men and women who can disguise themselves as an ashtray and kill you with a blow from their eyebrows. When you become aware of them hiding behind the potted plants – as I did once did during a meeting with Catherine Zeta Jones – it leads to a certain constraint.

It's unlikely you are going to reach across the table and grab the star by the throat but who knows what impulsive or ill-thought-out gesture or action will be misinterpreted. Keep your hands in sight all the time and make no sudden movement, is my advice or there may well be genuine bullet points in your presentation.

*

Los Angeles is a wild ride at the best of times. It's uncannily like the experience I underwent when I found myself strapped in the cockpit of a NASCAR racing automobile wearing anti-flammable overalls, gripping an absurdly small steering wheel at a NASCAR certified race track.

I was about to experience at first hand some of what it must feel like to be a professional racing driver because potentially I'd be writing a series involving a uniquely American spectacle. That means I needed to see what it involved not only technically but physically, mentally and emotionally.

The top drivers on the hottest tracks maintain *average* speeds of over a hundred and ninety miles per hour with their cars literally inches from each other. Imagination will do part of the work about what that means but to fully inhabit the characters you need to risk your own neck.

The morning had been spent in the classroom, reviewing the physics of high speed motion and its kinetic effects on the machine and, more importantly, the human body. Faced with the reality of the flimsy looking car itself all I could remember was that it was vitally important – as in Oh-my-God-I'm-going-to-die important – to accelerate into the corners and lift your foot off the gas as you came out of them. Or was it the other way around?

My survival in the minutes ahead would depend on understanding how to transfer weight between the front set of tires and the rear tires and on how securely Clem the instructor had strapped me into the cab. At maximum speed I'd be traveling almost the length of a football pitch every second so my hope was that he wasn't quite as laid-back as he seemed.

One thing Clem seemed to need to make sure I did understand was that in no circumstances was I to try to change gears or apply the brake. Gear shifts at the speed I'd be traveling had to be professionally handled, otherwise the entire transmission could disintegrate, sending shrapnel upwards through my seat.

Braking at hundred and eighty miles an hour could result in total loss of control of the vehicle, followed by a short flight and a heavy landing in the bleachers. Coming to a stop meant switching the engine off by the kill switch and coasting to rest a quarter mile later. The arrow pointing to the word KILL on the dashboard could, I thought, have been in a color other than blood red.

*

If donning the fire-proof overalls had been thought-provoking, the moment when my helmet was cinched tight on the straps which bolted it to the cockpit frame was truly sobering. The G-forces were going to be such that even in standard maneuver I could break my neck.

Clem came to life as he described what had happened to a friend of his who thought such a precaution too sissified. There were no rearview mirrors for reasons connected to the statistic about the football field above and through the goggles, already steamed up with perspiration, I seemed to be staring into a morning haze on the Dogger Bank in February.

I have pretty relaxed standards when it comes to windscreens. My demands are modest. No one has ever accused me of grand-standing about them. I just need to see through them. The one in front of me was made of plastic and to my troubled eye seemed to be covered with dead flies, streaks of oil, gouges, scratches and, just below my eyeline, a strip of duct tape.

Duct tape is ominous at the best of times. It expresses both the urgent and the slap dash. Neither qualities you should be brooding about as last minute safety instructions are shouted at you and Clem checks the on-board fire extinguisher, the exact operation of which he seems puzzled by.

*

The next few minutes convinced me that I did not have a hidden talent for driving sheet metal at insane speed around an oval track whose corners are banked at thirty degrees, overtaking or being overtaken on both sides with inches to spare.

The series was never made. The plug was pulled even before we went to script because of insurance concerns. The whole thing, however, stands up pretty well as a metaphor not just for making your way in Hollywood but for a career in the arts in general. Your foot is on the gas; your gaze ahead is limited; you're taking the corners with a blind faith and unable to look in the rear mirror, brake or change gear until the work is completed.

You're also constantly having rivals whizzing past you or you are whizzing past them but your task is to stay on the track yourself, whatever they're up to. It's not the others you have to beat but yourself – which is something that can be hard to cling to in Los Angeles, the ultimate company town.

Pull up at a stoplight. There's a billboard dead ahead advertising a movie you haven't written. Look at the side of the thirty-two-ounce Slurpee you're about to drink. It's a promotion for a TV show you didn't produce. The radio is hosting an interview with an Academy Awards nominee who isn't you. The only people you know are also trying to make it in show business. Even more depressing than watching your friends struggle is hearing of their success.

All anyone wants to talk about are grosses, deals, who's just hit it big and who's been fired. The internet is a Babel of gossip, celebrity sightings, TV show and movie rankings that have only one thing in common – it ain't about you.

Back home in Skull Creek, Indiana – or Coventry, England – this might not be so hard to bear. In LA it's happening all around you.

Everybody in the coffee shop is writing a movie. Even the valet parking guy is working on a pitch.

I was lucky. I wrote only on commission. I had a body of work and an agent from one of the top agencies. Even so, there was that constant bombardment of reminders of the stuff I wasn't writing, that I was very definitely not involved in that was making millions – *millions!* – for somebody else. How much worse had it to be for somebody who really was clinging to the iceberg by their fingertips and slipping remorselessly into the icy water.

*

The Emmy was a great lifebelt, of course. It's virtually a guarantee of five years' work. Nominations and awards for that work took me to the Emmys several more times as well as the Golden Globes.

There's much to savor for the sharp eyed at these School Prize Days and not just the rictus grin of the sore losers. The producers of these events are anxious that the shots of the audience contain no empty seats. These affairs, especially the Oscars, are trumpeted as pillars of communal civilization.

If the viewer at home sees acres of upturned seats they are going to question the cosmic importance of it all so a few dozen Screen Actors Guild members are paid to hover in the foyer in rented tuxes and ball gowns. They are hurled into the breach during commercial breaks, when the stars head for the toilets.

Yes, Virginia, even movie and TV stars poop.

For many of whom this will be the apogee of their careers. In years to come their grandchildren will cluster around them in Sioux Falls or Parsippany begging to be told yet again whose bum marks in the velour they perched on, so brutal and unforgiving a career in show business can be.

*

I don't wish to strip away anyone's illusions but the rigmarole of secrecy surrounding whose name is actually in the totemic envelope is, at least sometimes, in the Irish vernacular, a bit of a cod.

My first Emmy nomination arrived so soon after my move to Los Angeles that I was still unaware of what a big deal it was. Renting a tux would put a dent in the budget at a time when it was still uncertain how long I could remain. I was currently staying on the beach but living on the stones was a distinct possibility.

The studio PR team leant heavily on me when I communicated that I might be a No Show. *You have to go,* they said, with a conspiratorial wink. *It will be worth your while.* They pretty much indicated not that the fix was in but that they knew from the tellers who had won the screenwriting horse-race.

It *was* worth my while because winning something like an Emmy pretty much guarantees you several years-worth of work. Even if you serially screw up, bankrupt the companies you work for and destroy the careers of every actor involved in your projects, hey, they still can't take it from you.

The purpose of this book is to make sure you don't need a book like this. Which means that success will come your way and when it does you'll have to learn how to handle celebrity, attention and fame. For writers, I hasten to add, there will be a relatively modest amount of all those things. That's just how it is. But still. You should know how to prepare for it.

When Johnny Carson was asked to come up with the least likely sentence to have been spoken in human history he suggested *That's the banjo player's Rolls Royce.* A close second might have been *There's the famous screenwriter whose name the crowd is screaming.* We labor mostly unseen and in the shadows and probably we prefer it there but now and again you'll see your name in lights.

I've looked at mine on a fifty-foot-high poster on Sunset Boulevard; outside a West End Theatre and theatres in New York and spelled out in giant LEDs moving across the frontage of the National Theatre. I've seen it – and myself – on TV interviews and in the pages of newspapers and magazines.

I'm here to tell you that, when you see yours in an odd but very real way it won't have anything to do with you. You won't feel a surge of emotion or wet yourself with excitement. Your struggles won't flash in front of your eyes and the Universe won't shout *Yes!* The Universe will stay pretty quiet about the whole thing in fact because the name attached to the movie or TV show or play doesn't really belong to you.

The entity which wrote that script or screenplay is the one who figures in Henry James' short story about the admirer of a prominent author who watches him in a hotel restaurant one night. With the great man still holding forth at the table, the narrator has occasion to go upstairs. The door to one of the bedrooms is open and there is the exact double of the writer bent at his task, covering sheet after sheet of paper.

*

Then there's the fans and well-wishers. Sometimes the stiletto blade is hidden in the bouquet. I've come to mistrust anyone who grabs me by the hand after a premiere or first night and pumps it up and down while repeating *That was unbelievable.* An equally subtle put-down is the steady look in your eye and the words *I don't think you could write a better movie.*

The full-out attack is on the whole easier to take. At least it's honest. At the party to celebrate one of my first nights someone cornered me and rattled off a list of everything I'd written to date. It looked to her, she said, as if here at long last was a contemporary Irish writer to stand alongside Synge and O'Casey.

Lulled by this I prepared to bashfully shrug off the crowning compliment. Instead she told me with some venom that the show she'd just seen blew up any chance of that. *You might as well keep working in television. When it comes down to it you're just a bloody soap opera writer.*

Ouch.

15

CITY OF NETS

Bertolt Brecht was also lured by that jeweled claw of Hollywood and tried to make his career as a screenwriter; having his *kuchen* and eating it, too. Otto Freidrich used the words above as the title of his book on Hollywood in the 1930s and 1940s, which is also required reading.

The exiled Brecht was dazzled by The Silver Screen and Tinseltown, as were so many European intellectuals. The house I lived in first in Los Angeles was very near the one Brecht stayed in, hoping to break into the movie business as yet another in the long line of freeloading chancers drawn by the tinkle of coin.

He was deadly serious about it and took the studio system on its own terms. When walking nearby, I always took a detour to that street and ran my hand along the garden railings.

Writing is a lonely profession on the whole, although the collegiate, collaborative nature of writing scripted drama means you have to be a kind of gregarious hermit. Now and again it's heartening to see the port or starboard light of another writer off the bow as you chug through the night, hoping for landfall.

There have been others out here, ploughing the waves and it's oddly reassuring to catch a glimpse of them. For me most of them have been accidental sightings and each has carried something of their own personality.

Walking on the cliffs near Boscastle in Cornwall, for example, I fell into conversation with an old but still sprightly farmer who, when he found out that I was a writer, said that when he was a young boy a famous writer had been pointed out to him in the village.

He couldn't remember the name but he'd written a short story set on a nearby cliff and had been the architect who had remodeled a church in the district. In disbelief I asked him if the name could have been Thomas Hardy. *That's it,* he said, then wrinkled his face. *He were a dirty bugger wi' women, I heard.*

In neighboring Devon, my brother had a friend in Torquay with a milk round. At one house a hand would appear when the milk was delivered at five every morning and an Irish voice call out from the bedroom window *Thank you, milkie.*

It was Sean O'Casey, come to Torquay to die but with a new-found kindness that carried him to the very end after the tumult of his professional and personal life. I shared this with the actor at Molly Malone's bar but he wasn't impressed. *Probably looking for a free pint of milk,* he sniffed.

In keeping with Joe Orton's black comedy I found myself talking to a London policeman in a bar, who said his sergeant had grabbed him when he was a raw constable and told him he was going to show him his first murder scene. On the way to it the sergeant warned that it was going to be bloody because it appeared to be a lover's quarrel, decided by a blunt instrument.

When they arrived at the flat where Orton lived with David Halliwell, his killer, things were indeed messy. The fresh-faced constable took off his helmet, went into the bathroom to throw up and came out to be told to pull himself together and help look for the murder/suicide note. *There's always a suicide note,* the gruff sergeant insisted but after a couple of hours close searching it couldn't be found.

The search was called off and the constable told he could go. When he picked up his helmet the note was underneath it.

In another pub I found myself talking to the owner of the bar where Flann O'Brien used to drink. I learned two things from him. First that if somebody looks as if they're about to cause trouble, check the size of their fists and how many scars are on them. That will tell you whether to hit them first.

The second was that the writer used to stand by himself in a quiet corner to drink but from time to time a smile would cross his face and he'd scribble something on a beermat. This would be turned into comedy for the next day's *Irish Times* or end up in one of his novels or short stories. *The thing is,* the ex-bar owner said slyly *he wasn't half as invisible as he thought he was.*

*

Many years of trying to puzzle out the exact meaning of that phrase have left me defeated. Deep questions are raised by the concept of being only fifty per cent invisible. Wouldn't that mean you were still completely visible? A small prize will be offered by the publisher to anyone who can nail it, although maybe all writers are trying to be invisible and only half succeeding.

In pre-war Hollywood there were those for whom Nazi dominated Germany and Austria were too dangerous to be seen in any way. This led to a well-documented exodus which gave the movie industry Billy Wilder, Greta Garbo's screenwriter, Salka Viertel (whose grandson I later worked with) and many other exiles such as Fred Zinnemann.

Then, as now, Los Angeles was a place where outsiders felt at home and could prosper – or alternatively sink without trace and end up toe tagged as John or Jane Doe in the County Hospital morgue. In the thirties, after an unusually egregious executive decision, Carl Laemmle was alleged to have snapped *From now on it's not just enough to be Hungarian to work at this studio. You also need to have talent.*

Heavyweight novelists like the Nobel Prize winning Thomas Mann moved to Los Angeles, along with his brother Heinrich, whose wife, a free spirited ex-barmaid, was given to opening the front door naked.

In *Joseph and His Brothers* Mann wrote *The storyteller's star is the moon. Lord of the road, the wanderer, the one who moves in his stations one after another freeing themselves from each.*

For the storyteller makes many a station roving and relating and pauses only tent wise awaiting further directions and soon feels his heart beating high partly with desire, partly too with fear and anguish of the flesh but in any case as a sign that he must take the road towards fresh adventures which are to be painstakingly lived through, down to the remotest detail, according to the restless spirit's will.

*

In the Manns' Los Angeles adventure they were in contact with other LA residents such as WH Auden, Christopher Isherwood and Aldous Huxley. Years later I was hired to work on a Huxley novel and discovered that the rights to the estate were owned by Sharon Stone. Yes, that Sharon Stone, a very smart woman indeed.

Thomas Mann lived in a large, splendid house in Pacific Palisades but once a week would make the drive, either along the beach by the Pacific Coast Highway or via meandering Sunset Boulevard, to the Farmer's Market at the corner of Third and Fairfax. A few steps, as it happens, from Molly Malone's bar. I have no evidence that the

Manns sank a pint there but it is on record that every Friday they would meet the other literary exiles in town.

The list included Leon Feuchtwanger, Franz Werfel and Bruno Frank and from time to time heavyweight musicians would drop by – Bruno Walter, Igor Stravinsky, and Arnold Schönberg. No doubt whistling one of their latest hits.

The boys met in the red banquettes at Du-Par's coffee shop and diner and one would have loved to be listening in when Brecht dropped by, an old adversary of the Manns. One would have relished even more being in even an imaginary meeting between Brecht and, say, Harry Cohn or Louis B. Mayer. He wasn't the first name you'd pick if you were looking to have the screenplay lightened up with a few gags.

*

There may be an existential reason why most writers most of the time prefer to keep their distance from other writers. Although it's reassuring to get those indications now and again across the waves that there are other vessels abroad, on the whole we prefer to travel alone and not in convoy.

There are few points of resemblance between myself and Virginia Woolf but I identify with her cautiousness about catching up even cursorily with the work of her contemporaries, let alone hanging out at the bar or dog track with them. If their stuff was brilliant, her thinking ran, how depressing. If it was rubbish it threatened to devalue the entire enterprise of art.

The countervailing argument would be Picasso's, who was once seen staring intently at a canvas in a host's house. Embarrassed, the owner insisted that he only displayed it as a whim of his wife's and that he was well aware it was a bad painting. *It's those you learn from,* Picasso replied.

Take your pick. Keep as much distance as you can between yourself and your fellow writers. Or hang out with as many as you can find and watch everything they write, good or bad.

*

Ben Hecht mined both *His Girl Friday* and *The Front Page* from events in a Chicago court house. On my way to rehearsals at The Goodman Theatre I always made a detour to touch the stonework. He authored, in *Child of the Century*, words about classic Hollywood which I framed and hung above my desk –

> *The loneliness of literary creation was seldom part of movie work. You wrote with the phone ringing like a firehouse bell, with the boss charging in and out of your atelier, with the director grimacing and grunting in an adjoining armchair.*
>
> *Conferences interrupted you, agents with dream jobs flirted with you, and friends with unsolved plots came in hourly. Disasters circled your pen. The star for whom you were writing fell ill or refused to play in the movie for reasons that stood your hair on end. The studio for who you were working suddenly changed hands and was being reorganized.*
>
> *This usually meant no more than the firing of ten or twenty stenographers but the excitement was unnerving. You listened to these alarms, debated them like a juggler spinning hoops on his ankles and kept on writing.*

I kept writing. I wrote in the canteen of a hospital where my first wife was undergoing a nine-hour brain operation. The night before the surgeon had told me that he could well kill her on the operating table, so difficult were the mechanics of this particular procedure and that I had better prepare myself and our two-year-old son for that outcome.

She survived. During those touch-and-go hours I worked on a situation comedy I had been commissioned for and the deadline pressed. Renoir was seen with his sketchbook and pastels at his father's deathbed. *How often do you get the chance to see the colors of a dying man's face?* he responded when taxed with insensitivity. Not quite the same thing, I know, but certainly in the ballpark.

I wrote the day after an earthquake had separated the staircase from the wall in the apartment in which I was living and there was a real possibility that the Fire Department would red tag it. I wrote during a Force Two hurricane in a beach house in the Caymans, where my foremost concern was trying to eke the laptop battery out, as all the power was gone.

I wrote when smoke hung in the air in the wildfire season, with one eye on the TV news because my in-laws were in the path of the advancing flames. They called and I drove to their house to help them evacuate, then drove back and picked up my writing where I left off.

I wrote with both arms in plaster after being attacked by two guard dogs who I was fighting off when the housekeeper walking them tripped in their leads. As she fell she landed on my chest and I broke both my wrists trying to mitigate the fall.

When I told this to the doctor who was setting the wrists he laughed so hard he mis-aligned the bones and six months later my right wrist had to be broken and reset. I wrote through that and through the difficulties of a double fracture of my elbow and in a cloud of Vicodin. I wrote when I felt too weak from pneumonia to lift my head from the pillow.

I wrote when I had food poisoning in Mexico and heat exhaustion in Morocco. I wrote in my hospital bed waiting for an operation to explore whether I needed a cardiac procedure. I wrote the day of my first colonoscopy when everything internal below my waist had been emptied out in a laxative-induced *tsunami*.

I wrote the day after receiving reviews of my plays or features or television series so savage and gratuitously insulting that they would fell an ox. In general I prefer not to read them at all. As a basketball player said *The highs ain't as high as the lows are low* and over the years I realized my skin wasn't thick enough to shrug off the bad ones or my self-respect so deficient that I needed praise.

*

I wrote and I kept on writing. My day began with breakfast in the Citrus Court of our Arts and Crafts house, restored from its previous incarnation as a crack house by the impeccable taste of my wife Alisa. For the underprivileged louts who have never had a Citrus Court it's an area demarcated by blood orange, satsuma, grapefruit, lemon, lime and kumquat trees, all beaming under a perfect sky.

From there I might saunter through one of the three gardens we had planted over the years, which sometimes featured on Los Angeles Garden Conservancy Tours. These are a kind of gardening Oscars. Sometimes I wondered if I shouldn't get them an agent and a manager.

One of the gardens was what the landscape architect who designed it called The English Garden and another was The Secret Garden and another was just, well, a garden but all of them were plangent with the sound of fountains and water features.

There was a koi pond and at one time I had hopes of training them to do what Winston Churchill did; when he appeared they swam to the surface to greet him. Mine dived to the bottom and hid. After heading into the huge, sun dappled kitchen with its butler's pantry I would make a cup of Jasmine Silver Needle tea – sip for sip more expensive than vintage champagne but probably the secret of eternal life – and head off to work.

*

My dad's journey to the building site was by bus, on foot or in the back of a truck but mine was a stroll to the Pool House, sided by glass and overlooking the swimming pool. It sat alongside thoroughbred shrubs with a *Ya looking at me, punk?* attitude.

We lived in a real neighborhood which controverted the idea of Los Angeles as a wasteland of unconnected suburbs where you only meet people when they mug you at the drive-up window at the bank.

Every day I went to my neighbor's porch at four sharp for an hour or two. He was an ex Los Angeles Police Department jailer who had locked up Sirhan Sirhan, The Night Stalker and Charles Manson, among others.

On an average day there would be anywhere between three and twenty people sharing the porch; dog walkers, other neighbors, passers-by, the local cops taking time out from patrol and conversation would range across topics such as the meaning of life and why the possum is the only mammal which can eat tin cans and is immune to rabies.

All this in usually perfect weather with the prospect of nothing but another perfect day ahead. As the bumper sticker says *Southern California – where it's never too late to have a happy childhood.*

I'm detailing the physical world of our corner of Los Angeles to hint at some of what we gave up when we moved to sixteen hundred square feet of Brooklyn. That restless, storyteller's spirit that Mann identified had to be listened to. I was comfortable in Los Angeles. Too comfortable to be comfortable.

I'd put roots as deep as you can in the desert sand in the westernmost edge of this extraordinary, hallucinatory country but now I was on the move again at a time when most people have fixed on where their journey will end.

Neville Cardus, the great English writer on both cricket and classical music wrote of Delius *There was nothing pitiable in him, nothing inviting sympathy in this wreck of a physique. He was wrapped in a monk-like gown, and his face was strong and disdainful, every line on it graven by intrepid living.*

Intrepid Living just about sums up the life of the artist, who needs to know when to stay and when to move on.

Exiled from Ireland, self-exiled from the England we'd then moved to, I'd ended up, despite its craziness, in a kind of earthly Paradise, Southern California but if I was to be true to the thing which had kept me grounded it was time to leave Eden again without one backward look.

I had managed to work in Hollywood for three decades on my own terms and, unlike so many, was leaving without a chip on my shoulder. This being Southern California of course that chip would have been organic, blue corn, gluten free, no added salt.

The moon beckoned. Time to fold up that storyteller's tent and go on the road again.

In the eighteen-seventies, Clinton Hill – where we've made landfall – was where the Irish who'd made a few dollars moved, something I discovered only after we bought the place.

Some years after it was built the diocese took it over. The five floors had been divided and subdivided into bedrooms – cells, really – for, over the years, literally hundreds of young Irishwomen shipped over from village and townland and the counties of Mayo and Connemara and Down and Donegal and elsewhere to this fearsome but exciting new world.

Faith, no doubt, brought many of them. Disappointment, others. Sheer survival some. Back then there were few men to be had at home due to endemic poverty and a flood tide of emigration that couldn't really be called a tide because tides pause and retreat and the flow of souls from Ireland never seems to cease.

My father, my mother, my brother, myself, had been part of one spill of people from a place too poor to support them. That history, that grievance, national and personal, had armed me for survival in a tough industry in a hard-nosed town.

A gift of the gab, a lively imagination, an eye for the main chance, a restless spirit, an understanding of the crucial part the subconscious plays in the working life of the artist and a belief that, if the world does in the end wear a tragic face, that's what the mask of comedy is there for -- those had been what Ireland had gifted me. The rest was up to me.

I'll be back at my desk tomorrow.

Writing.

16

THE MAKING OF MONSTERS

Marlon Brando and the forty-million-dollar train wreck
of *The Island of Doctor Moreau*

By Ron Hutchinson

For John Frankenheimer

1930 – 2002

Readings from HG Well's *The Island of Doctor Moreau,* William Shakespeare's *The Tempest* and words spoken by other characters are in italics. They're spoken by the second actor.

When our ship was wrecked we took to the life raft. We drifted famishing and tormented by an intolerable thirst. After the first day we'd said little to each other and lay in our places and stared at the horizon or watched with eyes that grew more haggard every day the misery and weakness gaining upon our companions. The sun became pitiless. The water ended on the fourth day and we were already thinking strange things and saying them with our eyes but it was the sixth day before one of us gave voice to the thing we had all been thinking.

When they began to draw lots I sat in the bows with my clasp-knife in my hand although I doubt if I had the stuff in me to fight. They chose instead one of the sailors to be eaten. He was still strong. The others grappled with him. I crawled along the boat to help but the intended victim stumbled and fell overboard with one of his attackers. They sank like stones. I remember laughing at that and wondering why I laughed. The laugh caught me suddenly like a thing from without.

Soon the others all died or leapt overboard. I survived and was rescued by a schooner that had no business in these remote waters. One night land was sighted after sundown. It was too far to see any details; a low-lying patch of dim blue in the uncertain blue-grey sea. An almost vertical streak of smoke went up from it into the sky. It was low and covered with thick vegetation. The beach was of dull grey sand and irregularly set with trees and undergrowth.

I fancied that I saw some grotesque-looking creatures scuttle into the bushes. I heard cries of an exquisite expression of suffering as if all the pain in the world had heard a voice. In spite of the brilliant sunlight and the green fans of the trees waving in the soothing sea-breeze the world was a confusion, blurred with drifting phantasms.

*

While working at Dreamworks I turned down the chance to rewrite *Gladiator*, because I thought it ridiculous and had no chance of making money. I did, however agree to work on one of the great movie disasters of all time; one so legendary that at least one documentary has been made about the debacle. The movie is an adaptation – I'll explain in a moment what Hollywood means by that word – of HG Wells' novel about a renegade scientist who creates an island of monsters, which New Line Cinema were to shoot in the rain forests of Northern Australia. We could have shot in Hawaii or on a back lot or in the Pasadena Botanical Gardens, come to that, but there's still a tough guy swagger to many in Hollywood, especially when it comes to choosing locations.

Some of this swagger has to do with the outlaw past of The Big Avocado, when at any time the shooting of the first silent movies could have been interrupted by a visit from Edison's men looking to enforce his patents. The company would then skedaddle to the Mohave or Mexico to lie low until the heat was off.

The only place to compare with the physical hardships of this location, for me, was the shoot for HBO's *The Burning Season* in Chiapas, Mexico. There was an armed insurrection going on around us but what really did the damage was the culinary specialty of a snail the size of a soccer ball, hauled from the local lakes where the inhabitants washed their laundry and dumped, we discovered, their raw sewage.

This tasty treat felled the crew in waves, myself not excepted. I have a vivid memory of the taps running dry in the bathroom where I had spent an entire day on the floor wishing for death during one particularly severe tsunami of stomach trouble.

This is all to establish that I was no pushover when it came to challenging locations. Or to awkward customers in the workplace, such as movie stars with cosmic senses of entitlement, like Elizabeth Taylor. By the time I got to Australia I was versed in the manifold lunacies of the screen trade – superstars whose every appetite had to be indulged, producers who needed to be a combination of spoiled baby and homicidal maniac to cope with the pressures of their daily schedule and directors whose tantrums made you suspect that directing a movie wasn't a job description but a personality disorder.

In Brando – our star – I was about to find something new – an actor who hated acting and who had nothing but contempt for the business which had created him. An actor who seemed hell-bent on sabotaging the entire enterprise which in some circles is a cult movie for all the wrong reasons. You can catch it at midnight matinees, usually in college towns, where it's greeted, I imagine, with hoots of disbelief.

*

The walls of my apartment in Hell will be covered by the bad notices for it and it will be playing endlessly on the television there although, as you'll hear, not one word that I wrote appears on screen even though I got official screenplay credit. This is due to the vagaries of the credit arbitration system, a subject of Talmudic complexity. Claiming – or being damned with – any kind of credit on this one is a little like being given credit for malaria. On the other hand, screen credit determines who gets residuals, which over the years, even on something which swept the board in that year's Razzies for worst movie and actors, mount up.

The questions before us are how could some of the biggest talents in Hollywood – Marlon Brando, Val Kilmer, the director John Frankenheimer – get it so spectacularly wrong and how could a hard-nosed production company like New Line Cinema contrive to blow it on a scale which derailed the careers of several of those involved? Even more puzzling – how could it blow it on that scale and so many people keep their jobs?

Adapted From and *Based on,* by the way, usually mean the studio is using the title and throwing the rest of the book away after a quick read. If they even bother to read it at all. It's the same way *A true story* usually means a bunch of lies the screenwriter has made up. The core of this story – which you can't really fundamentally tinker with – is HG Wells' novel from 1896, a period when there was much discussion about both the good and the bad uses of science; especially in the light of Charles Darwin seeming to blur the distinctions between the animal kingdom and ourselves.

Having trained as a biologist Wells writes of the island and its inhabitants – human and animal or in the form of the Beast People shaped by Moreau's scalpel into something that is both and yet neither with an obsessive intensity –

> There was a rustling amid the greenery on the other side of one of the streams. Something appeared. At first I could not distinguish what it was. It bowed its head to the water and began to drink.
>
> A man, going on all fours like a beast.
>
> His eyes met mine. Forthwith he scrambled to his feet and stood wiping his clumsy hand across his mouth. He slunk away and, crossing the stream I found a great patch of vivid scarlet on the ground, the body of a rabbit with its head torn off. The thicket about me became altered to my imagination. Every shadow became something more than a shadow, became an ambush; every rustle became a threat.

*

The first attempt to make this movie here with this team had been in effect a shipwreck that went down with pretty much all hands. The director Richard Stanley's ambition had been to make a movie that would pay homage to what he thought of as the great Japanese science fiction movies of the 1950s. After months of preparation he was fired after three days' shooting. He and his guys were out and John Frankenheimer and his team – including me – in. Just like that. Hollywood could teach Darwin a thing or two about survival of the fittest.

When the call from John came – we had already worked together on several Emmy-nominated projects and a couple of movies – I was flown from London, where I'd been in rehearsal on a stage play.

En route I stopped off in Los Angeles for a day in which I did my laundry and fitted in a minor car accident with a guy called Earl at an LA gas station. Earl, buddy, I should have realized you had been sent by the Fates to stop me getting on that plane. As I took my First Class seat – as per the Writers Guild of America West minimum basic agreement – I was happily unaware this was a kamikaze mission that I'd be lucky to escape from with my career intact.

Seventeen pampered hours to Sydney. A three-hour layover. Then a couple of hours to Cairns, the other end of Oz, next stop Papua New Guinea. Cairns – locally pronounced Kens – gets six foot of rain a year, the bulk of it in the months we'd be shooting there and is the gateway to the Great Barrier Reef.

It's a fabulous place to see a lot of droppings from fruit bats and toucans and if you're into mud flats, Downtown's the place for you, it's built on one. Outside is triple canopy jungle and sugar cane and – well, we'll let the location safety manager's briefing speak for itself. It's the one he gave me before he'd even let me out of the four by four he drove me to the set in –

> *In a nutshell it's fair to say that every indigenous form of Australian wildlife is lethal, mate. It can bite you, sting you, claw you to pieces or kick you to death. Driving at night is a No-No due to the possibility of collision with emus and cassowaries, who tend to congregate on the highways and seem to be made of pre-stressed concrete. There are also an estimated hundred thousand camels running loose in the outback and on no account drive over anything that looks like a piece of pipe. Sometimes it turns out to be a snake which will wrap itself around the wheel arch and treacherously strike as you got out of the vehicle later.*

The sugar industry had added to the hazards several years previously by importing cane toads to control the rodents which ate the sugar cane. Over time they had become a problem in their own right.

> *Not only are they ugly sons of bitches which weigh in at around two pounds, they disable their prey by spitting poison in its eye. When cornered they will do that to humans, too. And watch out for the jellyfish.*

Millions of deadly box jellyfish descend on the nearby waters by the millions to breed at that time every year. You do not want to mess with sex-crazed jellyfish. Instead of shooting on a beach near Cairns we shot on another one conveniently situated on a crocodile-infested island a two-and-a-half-hour boat ride away.

My accent puzzled the safety guy.

Are you a Pom?

I said I was born in Ireland yes but now lived in the States.

So you're a Seppie, then?

I guessed I was. It was only later that I found out that to the crew Americans were Septic Tanks – Yanks – in rhyming slang. Where this hostility came from I have no idea. It added another level of tension to daily life and later would have, literally, explosive consequences.

*

Cairns' international airport had only recently opened and opened mainly to funnel customers to the Cairns casino. There was still much of the outback here. Meat pie with chips was on every menu. There were no chairs in the local bars. Too readily used as weapons in the frequent fights. You drank standing up or leaning on posts. Val Kilmer had taken to wearing a robe or male sarong or – okay, yes, a dress – of a flowered pattern and went into one of the bars like that. He didn't stay long. The line producer rented a house on the beach until a ten-foot-long crocodile chewed its way through the screen door while his wife was feeding their three-month-old infant. This is not the Australia of Bondi Beach. On a week off some of the crew loaded up a couple of jeeps and drove into the triple canopy jungle to explore. They covered only twenty miles in five days and came back covered in insect bites and in much the same condition Alec Guinness is in when he exits the sweat box in *Bridge On The River Kwai*.

Wells had never been to Cairns or a rain forest but he imagined it pretty well when his narrator goes Walkabout –

> I emerged upon an open space surrounded by a dense growth
> of stems and twining vines and splashes of fungus and flowers.
> Before me, squatting together upon the fungoid ruins of huge
> fallen trees were three grotesque human figures but each of
> these creatures despite its human form and rags of clothing
> had woven into it – into its movements, into the expression
> of its countenance, into its whole presence – some irresistible
> suggestion of a hog, a swinish taint, the unmistakable mark of
> the beast.

A shipwreck. Rescue. An island. A sorcerer who rules the island. A monster. Sound familiar?

> Ye elves of hills, brooks, standing lakes and groves,
> And ye that on the sands with printless foot
> Do chase the ebbing Neptune and do fly him
> When he comes back –

There are other, previous footsteps on the dull grey sand of Wells' beach and not just Shakespeare's in *The Tempest*. Thomas Moore invented the island of Utopia to explore a vision of how we should order our affairs, the Chinese have their Peach Blossom Spring and the Germans Schlaraffenland – although you should not attempt to pronounce this at home.

Moreau's island is more Dystopia than Utopia, a reflection of its owner's dark past which had led to his flight from England –

> *A wretched dog, flayed and otherwise mutilated escaped from Moreau's house. He was already well known for his extraordinary imagination and a brutal directness. Some of his experiments were claimed by his own laboratory assistants to be wantonly cruel. Moreau was howled out of the country.*

Wells had been a biologist and had no doubt seen living flesh experimented on. That might inform the intensity of his writing –

> *There was blood, I saw, in the sink, brown and some scarlet and I smelt the peculiar odor of carbolic acid. Through an open doorway beyond, in the dim light of the shadow I saw something bound painfully upon a framework, scarred, red and bandaged and then blotting this out appeared the face of Moreau, white and terrible.*

> *Something cold touched my hand. I started violently and saw close to me a dim pinkish thing looking more like a flayed child than anything else in the world.*

> *What was it? What were they all?*

> *There was one experiment, a limbless thing that writhed along the ground. It was immensely strong and in infuriating pain. We hunted it. It killed one of our men. When his body was found one of the barrels of his gun was twisted into the curve of an S and very nearly bitten through.*

> *Moreau had made over a hundred creations not counting the smaller monstrosities which lived in the undergrowth and were without human form. They sometimes bore offspring but most*

of those generally died. When they lived Moreau took them and stamped the human form upon them.

Wells would have been aware of a theory then fashionable, that *Ontogeny recapitulates Phylogeny* meaning – pay attention, class – that the development of an organism – ontogeny – expresses all the intermediate forms of its ancestors throughout evolution – phylogeny. Thus the gill-like appendages of the infant in the womb are an echo of our remote past as fishy-wishies, for example.

My wife worked with a director who also had a scientific background who extended the theory to suggest that the experience of making a movie eerily replicates what the movie's about. If it's about betrayal, there'll be more than the usual number of back-stabbings, dirty work and defenestrations off screen. If it's a romantic comedy, the bedsprings will bounce red hot. If it's about the making of monsters – hang on to your hats.

There's no doubt there was some very odd behavior on the part of the crew and actors who had been on the location for several weeks by the time I got there. Richard Stanley, for example, the re-directed director, had surfaced again and refusing to accept it was no longer his movie, viewed dailies smuggled to him in his hotel room. They can't have been to his liking. John Frankenheimer was not somebody who intended to shoot a homage to classic Japanese science fiction films. He liked to work in the seam where entertainment met politics in movies such as *The Train, The Birdman of Alcatraz, Seven Days in May* and *Seconds*. That makes a heart-stopping list if you love movies.

Then there was *The Manchurian Candidate* which is about a plot to kill the President and came out in 1962. Jack Kennedy died the next year. John was great friends with Jack's brother Robert Kennedy, who was killed six years later. John drove him to the Ambassador

Hotel that night. Bobby, as John always called him, was staying out at Malibu with him. One of the political staffers took John aside –

> *Bobby's going to exit through the kitchen to shake a few hands. Meet him out back with the car.*

Sirhan Sirhan was waiting in the kitchen with a gun and as John tried to get to the back of the hotel moments later, not knowing what had happened, heard a newsflash –

> *Senator Robert Kennedy and several other people have been shot in Los Angeles and the dead includes his close friend, movie director John Frankenheimer –*

In a daze John drove back to Malibu. The FBI beat him to it and removed anything to do with RFK, including his dog. John believed that somehow *The Manchurian Candidate* had released some bacillus, some madness, something sinister into the America polity and went into a cocaine and booze inflected nose dive that last almost twenty years.

*

I got this directly from him, sitting in his trailer waiting for the shot to be lit in the course of the six or seven projects I made with him. His movie reputation was still there but nobody was going to take a chance on the other reputation. Home Box Office came to the rescue. He was offered a couple of jobs on anthologies like *Tales From The Crypt*.

Nothing against that show but John had directed Burt Lancaster, Warren Beatty, Frank Sinatra, Janet Leigh, Angela Lansbury and Laurence Harvey. There was also a version of *Breakfast at Tiffany's* he was due to shoot with Marilyn Monroe but the deal fell apart. Bob

Cooper, head of HBO offered him a chance to climb out of the crypt with a TV movie I was writing based on the Attica prison riots.

Sharing the plane ride to Nashville, where we were to shoot in a jail, John told me he had to get this right. If he blew it he was through.

The shoot was a tough one. At one point he needed a police bodyguard because some of the ex-cons working as extras took exception to how he spoke to them. For John, directing was a contact sport. That movie we made in Nashville, *Against the Wall,* won John his first Emmy in what would be a consecutive row of five.

Now I think about it, the upcoming clash between John and Brando was something like a classic Japanese science fiction film in which Godzilla battles another monster like Barugon or Gigan or Mothra, a giant moth which uses its wings to flap wave energy at its enemies.

I'm using monster in one of its early definitions –

Something extraordinary or unnatural; an amazing event or occurrence; a prodigy, a marvel.

John fit the bill on every account. In his twenties in the United States Air Force, Curtis Le May – who firebombed Japan and organized the Berlin Airlift – spotted something in him and told him he'd become the youngest general in history if he stayed in the service. Instead John went into television. Shows were live back then and the pressure on the director in the booth immense. When one of them fainted from the stress John stepped in and calmly called the shots.

Calling the shots was something he did in every way. I can't count the number of times I heard him tell an executive –

You're confusing me with somebody who gives a shit.

Or –

If you ask me to see things your way, who's seeing them my way?

He insisted on total control of his projects, the way it used to be when you were the director, and at six foot five and such an athlete that he could have had a pro tennis career not many people cared to get in his way. He liked loud bangs and blowing things up. When the day players failed to give him the facial reactions he wanted, he had the armorer fire off a clip from an AK47 behind them.

That was a favorite trick to keep people on their toes. Shooting *Grand Prix* in England he'd actually blown up the tea wagon to get the extras' flagging attention. The British love their tea and biscuits. That's a surefire way to get them in line.

In Brando he was coming up against someone who also liked total control and could be even more of a monster. Fitting that what many saw as a slugfest between Frankenheimer and Brando should take place on a movie predicated on another definition of monster –

A mythical creature, part animal and part human, or combining elements of two or more animal forms. Frequently of great size and ferocious appearance.

*

The task of creating our screen monsters was in the hands of the legendary Stan Winston. Some of these effects were so complicated that it was necessary to have someone inside the costume working the levers and switches. In London I'd viewed several cassette tapes which John sent in advance of my arrival to let me know what I was in for.

They consisted of ninety minutes of Marlon Brando lying in a hammock with a very small person on his chest singing 'Frog Went A-Courting' to him. *Hmm.* When I say small person I mean someone who had to be carried around the set in a child's car seat in case he got stepped on. Nelson de la Rosa from the Dominican Republic, at just under twenty-eight inches tall – check it out in Wikipedia – was one of the smallest men ever measured. As soon as Brando set eyes on him he – well – he fell in love.

A sweet, sweet guy, Nelson became, for Brando, the heart of the movie. If you know your Hollywood trivia, their on-screen relationship was the inspiration for Mini-Me in Austin Powers. Was there method in Brando's madness or madness in The Method? Or was he just having a vacation at the production company's expense, the price being the chore of standing in front of the cameras now and again?

The craziness continued when Richard Stanley took to disguising himself as an extra and turning up on the set each day. An unusual state of affairs! He was however a direct descendant of Henry Stanley, whose epic search for the missing missionary David Livingstone resulted in one of the great lines of history –

Doctor Livingstone, I presume.

I wish I'd written that.

*

Brando.

He'd arrived on location weighing around three hundred pounds, most of it pizza and ice cream. Not in the best shape of his life. In the flesh – and there was a lot of it – he looked even more like all the vices of the dodgier Roman Emperors rolled into one but as someone said to me, on one of the rare occasions he left his trailer –

Look at him move. No one has ever moved so beautifully.

It was true. There was – I'm tempted to say an animal grace there but that would be lazy. Besides, we had a cat once who kept falling off things and missing them when he jumped at them. Brando's walk wasn't a swagger, it wasn't a statement – it just seemed to be that all the parts worked smoothly together and even if you didn't know who he was –

Charisma was originally a theological term, meaning divinely conferred power or talent. He had both so when he took one look at the original script and threw it out – and then when he placed a kitchen colander on his head, slathered himself in sunscreen, fell in love with Nelson, retired to his trailer and refused to leave it –

One of the ways in which he'd expressed his disdain for making movies was refusing to learn his lines. Even back in *The Godfather* days he'd read them off large posters attached to the other actors, turning them into walking billboards and ambulant teleprompters. Perhaps when you've spoken the liquid gold of Tennessee Williams everything else is mashed potatoes but –

In London I'd read the book. Some of Wells' writing in the run-and-gun sections is perfunctory. He comes to life in the arguments over ideas, such as that between Moreau and the narrator, once he'd understood the full, untramelled horror of what Moreau was up to –

I don't understand. Where is your justification for inflicting all this pain? The only thing that could excuse vivisection to me would be some application –

To which Moreau's chilling reply is that a mind opened to science must see that pain is a little thing. No one could imagine the strange, colorless delight of his intellectual desires, in which he longs to find out the limits of what can be done with a living shape.

The thing is an abomination, Moreau.

With a shrug Moreau accepts that the study of Nature makes a man at last as remorseless as Nature but –

— for the first time he looked troubled as he told me that somehow he always fell short of the things he dreamed. He could get the human shape out of the animals but often had trouble with the hands and claws. Not even his tolerance for the pain in his creatures could guarantee success. Somehow, too, he could not breed or inflict intelligence and there was somewhere he could not find or touch — the seat of the emotions. Each time he dipped a living creature into the bath of burning pain he swore that this time he would make a rational creature, free of it but each time failed.

If you can't get a good scene out of that you're not trying so I sent a few pages to John based on it. He liked them but told me he'd never be able to persuade Brando to say a word of them. According to Brando —

This isn't a movie. It's a pageant.

What does that mean, John?

Your guess is as good as mine.

There would also be a technical issue shooting any scene involving Brando and most of the other actors. Relations between them were by now poisonous. One actor had deliberately spoiled another's take by holding the tip of his cigarette to the focus puller's ear. The same actor had interrupted a scene to answer a mobile phone. Getting them to do something as simple as sit around a table was impossible.

Should it be necessary to shoot such a scene they'd do it one at a time and somehow the conversation would be glued together in post-production. No doubt this would lead to, shall we say, a little jerkiness in editing and odd eyeline effects but it would be the best that could be done.

The laws of libel caution me against a fuller description of the issues we had with the cast but as a sampler the armorer was so alarmed by one of their behaviors that he refused to allow him to handle even a blank firearm. A quick rewrite gave all the gunplay to another actor who promptly went horse riding, fell and shattered his femur.

He was now in plaster and could be shot only from the waist up. We already knew we'd be asking a lot of the audience but to have them swallow that a lead character had been suddenly and inexplicably crippled between one scene and the next and that, if he was to chase the rampaging Beast Men around the island with a gun, somebody was going to have to push him in a wheelchair –

You get the idea. Another day, another rewrite.

Given all this, the production might as well fall in line with Brando's insistence that he be allowed to improvise. As soon as he did that, the others followed suit. As a writer of course I'd naturally be against that. When one character asks another what Moreau's Nobel Prize was for, the answer comes –

He invented Velcro.

It's kind of funny but I'm not sure a writer would have got it past Quality Control. An actor can get away with it because once the cameras are rolling, the power is theirs.

*

Power.

Until the movie is green-lit the writer has it. He or she may be an ink stained wretch but nothing can happen without the scenario. As soon as its handed over – zip – the writer's power has gone. After the producer has put the money together and cast the show and found the director – zip. They're pretty much in the hands of the director who's in the hands of the star and if the star stays in their trailer, nothing is getting done and the studio is in meltdown.

The standing cost of us all being here, the other side of the world, with a small army of people to be paid, sheltered, flown in, flown out, costumed, haired and made up, with sets built or building and transport to be found, hotel rooms to be booked, location catering laid on, trailers to be rented, blocks of portable toilets hired and emptied, extras to be found, script sides to be printed, distributed, cancelled when a rewrite comes down, cameras to be at the ready, light poles, screens, the sound cart at hand, boxes and boxes of lenses, miles of film stock to be shipped back to LA with a dozen Customs forms to be completed for every single inch – we're burning through how much a day – fifty, sixty, a hundred thousand dollars and it's not as if you can totally concentrate on your job because what about that crocodile which chewed its way through the screen door of the house you rented on the beach and nearly snacked on your newly born and maybe your wife too – got to get them out, find somewhere safer or maybe accept that this island of Doctor Moreau, of Prospero and Ariel and Caliban is not a place for them –

> *Where should this music be? i' the air or the earth?*
> *It sounds no more: and sure, it waits upon*
> *Some god o' the island. Sitting on a bank,*
> *Weeping again the king my father's wreck,*
> *This music crept by me upon the waters,*
> *Allaying both their fury and my passion*
> *With its sweet air: thence I have follow'd it,*
> *Or it hath drawn me rather. But 'tis gone.*
> *No, it begins again.*
> *Full fathom five thy father lies;*
> *Of his bones are coral made;*
> *Those are pearls that were his eyes:*
> *Nothing of him that doth fade*

CLINGING TO THE ICEBERG

> *But doth suffer a sea-change*
> *Into something rich and strange.*
> *Sea-nymphs hourly ring his knell.*

There *was* something rich and strange here, in this place at the far side of the world. There were grotesque-looking creatures scuttling into the bush or feeding themselves at the craft services table. Here indeed there be monsters and the biggest of them, in both senses, that of –

> *Something extraordinary or unnatural; an amazing event or occurrence; a prodigy, a marvel.*

And –

> *A mythical creature, part animal and part human, or combining elements of two or more animal forms. Frequently of great size and ferocious appearance.*

– is lurking in his trailer-cave, Bud from Omaha, whose mom was a drunk and who hated his dad; Marlon Brando, on whom everything depends and that depends on the result of the battle of wills between him and John if only John can get him out of that damn trailer.

*

> *He was powerfully built with a fine forehead and rather heavy features but Moreau's eyes had that odd drooping of the skin above the lids which often comes with advancing years and the fall of his heavy mouth at the corners gave him an expression of pugnacious resolution.*

By this stage of his life Brando, playing the God of Moreau's island and emerging as the God of the production, was way beyond bored with show business and the making of movies. Overweight, unprepared, mocking, dismissive, on the razor's edge where caprice becomes malice – the case for the prosecution is therefore easily made. He was indeed here to sabotage this movie and what could John do about it? Wisely, as an old hand in show business, John ducked.

I'm here to direct Brando in a movie. That means my job starts when he exits the trailer. Getting him out of it is the producer's job.

When someone asked John why he'd taken the job on he said –

They offered me three million good reasons.

That money was in the bank whether Brando played ball or not, but the concern for the rest of us was that if our star brought this production down by caprice and obstructionism he'd inevitably harm our careers and reputations too. Hollywood is a small town. You might have had no part in the upcoming debacle but your name would be on the movie. Heck, they'd chisel *The Island of Doctor Moreau* into your tombstone and at your funeral service hand out the worst of the reviews.

What Brando was doing seemed to break the compact everybody in entertainment assumes we have with our audience. We'll give our best. Do our best work, every time. If the material is weak, we'll try to fix it. If we can't we'll still try to deliver.

I once saw Carol Channing at a two thousand seat theatre on a wet, miserable London evening. It must have been her god-alone-knows-how-many performance of *Hello Dolly*. She came on and her eyes flickered around the auditorium, counting the sparse house. Then she hit her mark, opened her pipes and gave it everything. At the curtain, after the applause died down – applause which in that massive theatre sounded like a few spots of light rain hitting a distant tin roof – she put her hand on her heart and breathlessly thanked us for being there, eyes sparkling, voice choking and totally sincere.

That's the deal, isn't it? The spectator, audience member, viewer – you out there – hands over good coin and we, in return, do our level best. Not to do that –?

*

What was John doing while Brando brooded, inhaled pizza or hid? He had other things on his plate. A raging feud, for example, with some of the Australian production people, burly and be-shorted. The sooner the show folded here in Kens, the sooner they could get out of the rain forest and back to Sydney. They could care less if Brando torpedoed the movie. The union had them covered.

One of the perks of the job would be divvying up the production furniture and effects, hand-made for the show with no expense spared. As soon as the sets were struck, they'd be whisked away. John got wind of it. He added a scene in which one of the renegade creatures seizes a gun and shoots up Moreau's house. Using live rounds and copious amounts of explosive squibs he reduced it and all the furniture and effects in it to matchwood, to the fury of the crew.

One of the pressures on him came from the studio. This was the early days of Computer Generated Animation. A large amount – five million dollars, maybe – had been spent on a scene in which mice with men's heads attacked somebody on a boat. It was never clear who that was or what the narrative point was meant to be but they'd spent all that money so –

Don't forget the Fighting Mice Men –

– was the cry from Los Angeles, in phone calls and by fax – daily, hourly –

Don't forget the Fighting Mice Men –

– haunted our dreams and even today when I meet another survivor of the shoot –

Don't forget the Fighting Mice Men –

– is the cry with which we greet each other.

*

And still, Brando is in his trailer. Brooding, it might be, on the king his brother's wreck, hearing those strange airs –

> *Full fathom five thy father lies;*
> *Of his bones are coral made;*
> *Those are pearls that were his eyes –*

– or just stuffing himself because who gives a damn if this movie gets made, if any movie gets made; it's years since he felt any passion for them or belief in what they can do and there is no more ridiculous and trivial way for a grown man to spend his life, Bud from Omaha especially, whose mom was a drunk and who hated his father.

Eventually our star emerged. He stood in front of the cameras and said the lines he chose to say. Some of these were relayed to him through a hearing device, it's claimed. One of his fellow actors says that now and again it would pick up police and emergency service transmissions and Brando would suddenly come out with *Armed robbery in progress at Woolworth's* or *Ambulance required at Woolagong Creek* in the middle of his dialogue because somebody had been carried off by a crocodile or attacked by a fruit bat. Anything was possible in Cairns. I still keep up with the news from there, by the way. The local paper recently carried a story about a thief who stole a parrot and replaced it with an almost identical parrot. The imposter had been stolen in its turn from somebody several miles away. That parrot had also been replaced with an almost identical parrot.

To date no ransom note had been received and the police are – wait for it – baffled.

Somehow John managed to get enough footage to cobble it together into a movie of sorts at a later date. There would always be loose ends in the story-telling – such as the Fighting Mice Men – but the job was done, despite crises large and small as constant as the ear-splitting shrieks of the toucans that infested the place – or how come the Puma Man walked upright yet had no visible genitalia.

Many tangled plot points were solved by the time-favored movie device of having a gasoline truck blow up in the climactic scene and it's fair to ask if any of us watching the fireball realized our careers were probably incinerated, too. The answer is No. In fact sketchy plans were being made for a *Return to the Island of Doctor Moreau* should it look as if we had a franchise here.

Inside the bubble of a production a weird optimism always seems to reign, in the same way no one has ever seen a bad set of dailies. This optimism lasted pretty much until the first previews, when the completed movie was first set in front of the public.

If you've ever been to Los Angeles you'll have seen haggard, blocks-long lines of studio audiences waiting in the broiling sun clutching their game show, chat show or sitcom tickets. There's no shade provided. No thoughtful distribution of bottles of water. The best condition for the mugs to be in, the studios long ago decided, is dehydrated and slightly off their heads with sunstroke.

In that condition anything is going to strike them as funny and they'll be too full of gratitude for the air conditioning which has saved their lives to be anything but appreciative of even the most witless drivel in which even at the best of times LA wades thigh deep. In my years there I often thought the bottom of the barrel had been scraped clean. Not so. There's always an eager executive able to spot something lurking there, reach into the gloop and bring something else to the surface.

Our proving ground was Camarillo, a couple of hours outside LA. It's a farming community in the main, which might explain its town website headlining a warning about the dangers of anti-coagulant rodenticides. I have no idea and neither do you what anti-coagulant rodenticides are but it sounds pretty bad.

Several hundred Camarillans had been – I guess the word is duped – duped into accepting free tickets for a sneak preview which was held on the studio meteorologist's advice on the hottest day of the year. Forced to wait for admission until done to a broil, they were plied with all the popcorn and free soda they could hold and then the movie was – shall we use the word *perpetrated* on them?

I was lurking at the back with John and some of the executives. It had never struck me before how expressive the backs of people's heads could be. Even their ears had something to say and it was soon clear it wouldn't be good. At the end it was obvious this wasn't going to be one of those moments when an audience holds its breath and then jumps to its feet, cheering. Many had jumped to their feet already and left, halfway through.

They'd all been given cards and pencils to rate the movie on. I hadn't paid much attention in school to negative numbers. It would have come in handy. The good folk of Camarillo were pretty much unanimously of the opinion they'd rather drink anti-coagulant rodenticide than sit through *Moreau* again. Or even once. I don't think it's ever been much fun living there but we'd brought them a whole new level of suffering.

The writing was on that improvised vertical writing surface, the wall. We didn't just have a flop on our hands. We had a catastrophe. Confirmation came with that ominous announcement in the review section of the newspaper *The studio has not released this movie for review.*

Pulling the print does however mean that the weekend audience is going to be blithely unaware that seeing it will be as bad for their health as French-kissing Typhoid Mary. You can grab some fast coin from the unsuspecting suckers and bank it before Monday rolls around so for a few giddy hours – say six pm Friday to midnight Sunday – we were the Number One movie in the US.

After that –

*

One could always hope, of course, that it might follow in the footsteps of other movies that were box office flops or critical duds when first released. *The Wizard of Oz*, for example, which was dead on arrival until it picked up some Academy Awards and *It's A Wonderful Life* which performed so woefully that the owners of the TV rights didn't even bother to renew them.

Nope.

That didn't happen and it's down to Brando. Right?

<u>The second actor becomes Brando, speaking from deep shadow, in Brando's own unique mocking, dismissive, seducing and flirting delivery, filled with pauses and odd rhythms, broken up by a verbal tic that sounded like *eh* which I'll leave for the actor to find.</u>

Is it possible – a modest enquiry – that Mr. Screenwriter here could be wrong? Mr. I'd-been-working-on-a-play-in-London-and-en-route-I-stopped-off-in-Los-Angeles-for-a-day-in-which-I-did-my-laundry-and-fitted-in-a-minor-car-accident-with-a-guy-called-Earl-at-an-LA-gas-station-and-Earl-buddy-I-should-have-realized-you-had-been-sent-by-the-fates-to-stop-me-getting-on-that-plane?

*Mr.Eventually-our-star-emerged-and-stood-in-front-of-the–
cameras-and-said-the-lines-he-chose-to-say-some-of-which-
were-relayed-to-him-through-a-hearing-device?*

*Could it be possible that instead of seeing the Marlon Brando
of his merry little tale as Moreau the God of the island who
ruled through cruelty and whim the scribbler should at least
take a moment to consider that the vrai Brando was more like
one of the hapless creatures sent to this outback Purgatory to be
experimented on? Could one not say that we actors, we mimes,
we puppets, we masquers are routinely required to offer ourselves
up with differing degrees of willingness to be operated on in a
procedure much like the high jinks Moreau gets up to in his lab?
Are we not – I ask in all modesty – asked to sew one patch of
living flesh – our own – to another in the process of creating a
character? Isn't that what the job is? And if that's so perhaps our
First-Class-Flying wordsmith might pause to reflect a moment
on the fear and pain involved?*

*Other pens than his of course had enjoyed themselves at my
expense. Mr. Roger Ebert, critic, for example, who had enormous
fun playing with himself on the page after my role in Don Juan
Demarco a few years before –*

*"Brando doesn't so much walk through this movie as coast,
in a gassy, self-indulgent performance no one else could have
gotten away with. Having long since proved he can be one of
the best actors in movie history, he now proves he can be one of
the worst. The problem with Brando these days is that we have
read so much about his acting techniques and shortcuts that it
is hard to see anything else. He adds little touches of business
and there are moments so bizarre that we wonder if the director
actually suggested them or whether Brando had a brainstorm
and everybody was afraid to tell him it wasn't such a hot idea.*

We can guess what the movie might have been like in the scenes where Brando is not around."

He might want to try to guess what some other movies might have been like without my Terry Malloy and Fletcher Christian and Don Vito Corleone and Colonel Kurtz — if anyone remembered those celluloid effusions sans moi. This one needs a Moreau but where do you find Moreau, a man who had made himself — well, yes, God of his own island? God who? God the Father? Should I base him on mine? Back in Omaha of course the old boy told me that I'd never amount to anything and didn't hang around to see, dumping us when I was eleven so you'll understand I don't really have — there's not much there to work with, is there?

Of course for those who believed the sun rose out of Mr. Lee Strasberg's fundament every morning, they'd no doubt suggest that old gasbag step forward for his bow but although he tried to take credit for teaching me how to act. He. Never. Taught. Me. Anything. He was an ambitious, selfish man who exploited people and tried to project himself as an acting oracle and guru. Some people worshipped him but I never knew why, it was Elia Kazan and Stella Adler who taught me to act but Elia or Stella as God?

Elia testified, named names, gave McCarthy's goons what they wanted and with Stella it was complicated so as always you're on your own, you are always alone, I learned that back in Omaha, with my dad who didn't like me and who drank as much as my mom who said she did like me but who liked boozing more so one thing we know about God is you can't tell him or her one damn thing, this is my house and you'll never amount to anything, you little smart-ass bastard and it's my way or the — that's right, the highway —

Instead of which it's papa who leaves and the survivors of my family disaster beach in Libertyville, Illinois where Bud here spends a couple years in a part-time job, usher, local movie theatre – don't stick gum on the seat-back, get your hand out of that girl's dress – and up there – up there – on that screen –

*

> *Be not afeard; the isle is full of noises,*
> *Sounds, and sweet airs, that give delight and hurt not.*
> *Sometimes a thousand twangling instruments*
> *Will hum about mine ears; and sometime voices,*
> *That, if I then had waked after long sleep,*
> *Will make me sleep again: and then, in dreaming,*
> *The clouds methought would open, and show riches*
> *Ready to drop upon me; that, when I waked,*
> *I cried to dream again.*

I had of course dreamed Terry Malloy and Fletcher Christian and Don Vito Corleone and Colonel Kurtz and gave delight to the world and now the new task ahead of me – perhaps it does start with saying It isn't a movie, it's a pageant and putting a kitchen colander on my head and slathering myself in sun screen and even, yes lying in a hammock for hours at a time trying to teach Nelson a song. Maybe something would come from that the way it had done so often, something instinctual and right, just right without explanation.

Mr. Ebert can amuse himself with 'there are moments so bizarre that we wonder whether Brando had a brainstorm' but at the end of the day it's not he who has to get inside the skin of a character who boasts that he began his experiments with a sheep and killed it after a day and a half by a slip of the scalpel and then took another sheep and made a thing of fear and pain and left it bound up to heal. Who says that it looked quite human to him when he had finished it and that it remembered him and was terrified beyond imagination and the more he looked at it the clumsier it seemed until at last he put the monster out of its misery.

It's not Good Ole Rog who will give us the Moreau who can boast of these things and sneer at what he sees as animals without courage, mere fear-haunted, pain-driven things without a spark of pugnacious energy to face torment and which are no good for man-making and man-making is what Moreau is after and we all agree I think that man-making is peculiarly God's business and maybe it takes a kind of genius to put a kitchen colander on your head when looking for a way to play him not from whim but hoping to find the moment when it all inexplicably, wonderfully comes together in that stroke of genius, the flash of inspiration, the sudden, swooping moment when the answer we've been looking for with our subconscious mind as well as our conscious one arrives when we find Grace, the opening up to the power of the irrational, a thing beyond simple explanation.

I would counsel my friend here as he plies his trade of supplying dialogue by the yard to the movie and TV business to bear in mind Maxim Gorky's maxim that the subconscious is the true hero of the imaginative life.

So perhaps and perchance that was what I waiting for when I seemed to be wasting everybody's time or making fools of them and perhaps and perchance when I looked at Nelson de la Rosa and saw the way in which Nature had made him it wasn't just caprice that made me ask him to climb into the hammock alongside me, sit him on my chest and teach a nonsense song to him.

*

The Beast People in the end turn on their God.

"The Leopard-man had risen from his knees and his eyes aflame and his huge feline tusks flashing out from under his curling lips leapt toward his tormentor. Only the madness of unendurable fear could have prompted this attack. The whole circle of threescore monsters seemed to rise about us.

The two figures collided. I saw Moreau reel back from the Leopard-man's blow. There was a furious yelling and howling all about us. The furious face of the Leopard-man flashed by mine. I saw the yellow eyes of the Hyena-Swine blaze with excitement. The Satyr glared.

I heard the crack of Moreau's pistol. I saw the Leopard-man strike him and now we were all running. Tongues lolling out, the Wolf-women ran in great leaping strides. The Swine folk followed and the Bull-men. I heard a cry behind me and turning saw an awful face – not human not animal but hellish, seamed with red branching scars, red drops starting out upon it and the lidless eyes ablaze, a monster swathed with red-stained bandages.

They rushed on, out of sight. Suddenly the morning was as still as death. Not a whisper of wind was stirring, the sea was like polished glass, the sky empty, the beach desolate. In the silence I heard a pistol shot, then a yelling cry and another dismal gap of silence.

Searching we found Moreau face downward. One hand was almost severed at the wrist and his hair was dabbed in blood. His head had been battered in by the fetters of the puma. We took his mangled body into the compound. Then we went into the laboratory and put an end to all we found living there."

Doesn't the spectator, the viewer, you – the Beast People of the audience – always expect the role of a lifetime from Brando and if you and Ebert R. don't get it you'll consign him to a similar end although even the most ingenious trouper has only a few faces in his or her pocket?

That I suggest is what Mr. Brando was struggling with during those long Antipodean days and longer nights with the production clock ticking, knowing that at some point he would have to leave his trailer and hope that when he put his hand in his pocket for another face there would be something there and not just the lining, lint and a stick of gum although one can hardly expect a mere word butcher to understand the pain and, yes, the fear involved in that.

*

The God that Brando eventually found is not – just as Wells' Moreau is not – a God of Love, no bestower of Hippy Dipshit Fairy Dust, he does not rule The Land of the Happy Pink Unicorns, this island is not a kind place, fear and pain rule here, the Beasts are kept in line by terror, dread of the door behind which is –

– blood, brown and some scarlet and a peculiar odor of carbolic acid and something bound painfully upon a framework, scarred, red and bandaged –

– on an island –

– where I heard cries of an exquisite expression of suffering as if all the pain in the world had heard a voice –

– ruled by a God whose creatures hiss and slobber through lips made by the surgeon's knife as they chant –

His is the House of Pain, His is the Hand that makes, His is the hand that wounds –

– the hand from which there is no escape as the Ape-man found –

I did a little thing, a wrong thing once. I am burnt. Branded in the hand.

– and no one ever, ever, ever leaves alive.

*

There's cruelty and threat on Shakespeare's imagined island, too. Prospero to Ariel, whom he's freed from her enchanted captivity –

> *Thou best know'st*
> *What torment I did find thee in; thy groans*
> *Did make wolves howl and penetrate the breasts*
> *Of ever angry bears: it was a torment*
> *To lay upon the damn'd, which Sycorax*
> *Could not again undo: it was mine art,*
> *When I arrived and heard thee, that made gape*
> *The pine and let thee out.*
> *If thou more murmur'st, I will rend an oak*
> *And peg thee in his knotty entrails till*
> *Thou hast howl'd away twelve winters.*

Ariel's torments, however, were rooted in Magic, not Science and Prospero's power is one that can be given up.

> *This rough magic*
> *I here abjure, and when I have required*
> *Some heavenly music, which even now I do,*
> *To work mine end upon their senses that*

This airy charm is for, I'll break my staff,
Bury it certain fathoms in the earth,
And deeper than did ever plummet sound
I'll drown my book.

If Science is about objective truth then there is no limit to the nightmare its misuse can plunge us into. That book can't be drowned.

Wells ends his with –

After Moreau's death and the destruction of the creatures being experimented on I constructed a raft and fled the island even though I had no desire to return to mankind. I was rescued at sea. I came eventually back to London. There I could not persuade myself that the men and women I met were not also another Beast People, animals half wrought into the outward shapes of human souls and that they would presently begin to revert, to show first this bestial mark and then that.

I know this is an illusion, that these seeming men and women, men and women forever, perfectly reasonable creatures, full of human desire and tender solicitude, emancipated from instinct are beings altogether different from the Beast Folk. Yet I shrink from them and it seems to me at times that I am not a reasonable creature but only an animal tormented with some strange disorder in the brain.

There is of course another island that you – me – all of us are on. Island Earth. This possibly not very unusual planet, given the millions or billions out there, circling a minor star on an insignificant arm of a galaxy that's like many, many others. Scientists, philosophers, futurologists, cosmologists, mathematicians and the guy in the bar will tell you that this little world of ours may not be all it seems. It may be a computer simulation or an experiment or a fiction – a short story some cosmic intelligence has devised to amuse itself.

We'd have no way of knowing that, any more than the creatures in Wells' novel were allowed to know they were artefacts of his imagination. It would spoil all the fun if they did. It would spoil the experiment – if that's what it is – for us to be allowed to be aware we're living in a giant test tube. If we are in the hands of some cosmic Moreau – well – the fear and pain of us, his Beast People, don't seem to matter much to him, do they, on the whole?

In *The Time Machine* Wells expresses a dark vision about the ultimate fate of Island Earth when he sends The Traveler into the far distant future –

I travelled, stopping ever and again, in great strides of a thousand years or more, drawn on by the mystery of the earth's fate, watching with a strange fascination the sun grow larger and duller and the life of the old earth ebb away. At last, more than thirty million years hence, the huge red-hot dome of the sun had come to obscure nearly a tenth part of the darkling heavens. Then I stopped once more. I looked about me to see if any traces of animal life remained but I saw nothing moving, in earth or sky or sea. From the edge of the sea came a ripple and whisper. Beyond these lifeless sounds the world was silent.

Silent? It would be hard to convey the stillness of it. All the sounds of man, the bleating of sheep, the cries of birds, the hum of insects, the stir that makes the background of our lives – all that was over. As the darkness thickened, the eddying flakes grew more abundant, dancing before my eyes; and the cold of the air more intense. At last, one by one, swiftly, one after the other, the white peaks of the distant hills vanished into blackness. The breeze rose to a moaning wind. I saw the black central shadow of an eclipse sweeping towards me. In another moment the pale stars alone were visible. All else was rayless obscurity. The sky was absolutely black and a horror of this great darkness came on me.

It's a vision of our collective future as terrible as that of the individual destinies of the beings in Moreau's hands – so terrible that it does seem to reduce us to animals tormented with some strange disorder in the brain. And yet – and yet there's something missing.

Moreau misses it when he pushes past his victims' pain and fear to locate the seat of emotion. He misses the gift we've been given to bear the bleakness of our future and for too many of us, our present. Wells ignores it in this book even though he showed he was a master of comic writing in his earlier *History of Mr. Polly* and *Kipps*.

Humor.

Believe it or not I think Brando possessed a good measure of it. It expressed itself in how he spoke, with a teasing, flirting, seducing mockery as if none of this was serious and we were all in on the joke and in his gift for mischief – playful misbehavior.

Play and misbehavior are both ways to overturn the ordinary, to get access to something deeper and unexpected, to rupture the membrane between the every-day and the sublime if only for a moment and we know it's that moment the creative artist is seeking, that flash of intuition, that stroke of genius – that zig zag stroke of lightning in the brain which defines greatness.

In its further meaning as a sense of the ridiculous it was there on the location when one humid, unbearably hot afternoon I got an urgent summons from an actor who was playing one of the pig-men or hyena-men, to go to his hotel room. Closing the door with a conspiratorial air he picked up his mask and lit a cigarette.

Watch this.

Placing the mask over his head he blew smoke down the snout. Quite a bit of it. Then took the mask off.

Did you see what I just did?

Er – yes.

It has to be in the movie.

It does?

Watch.

He put the mask on again and blew out more smoke.

Well?

It's – it's –

I wasn't quite sure what to do say, struck by the realization that the actor had been sitting in his room in front of a mirror for hours at a time for days, weeks or months on end trying to master this effect.

Can you write it in? Put it in a scene?

Ah –

Can you get it in the script?

Ah –

I want to say that his hand feverishly clutched mine but that's probably just a bullshit stage direction but he did say –

Tell John I can do this and it has to be in the movie. It just has to be.

And he blew smoke down his snout again.

Let's leave him and the whole experience there, with that imploring, desperate look in his eye, convinced that he had the magic key to unlocking a great movie, that if only that scene was included all would be well. A hundred million dollar opening weekend? Academy Awards including one for Best Performance By An Actor Wearing A Pig Mask?

New Line Cinema's *The Island of Doctor Moreau* cost forty million dollars to make and to date has returned around thirty million. Of course Hollywood accounting is more a matter of wishful thinking and outright fraud than simple arithmetic. Years later someone asked one of the executives what they'd really lost on the movie –

More than we'd have lost if we hadn't made it –

– was the first reply. When pressed to be serious –

Put it this way. We didn't lose as much on it as we'd have done if we'd lost more money on it.

'They didn't lose as much on it as they'd have done if they'd lost more money on it.' That's Hollywood thinking.

We're about done now and I'm not going to tell you if that scene finally made it into the movie and if it did if it's as great as the actor wanted it to be. To find out you'll have to rent, buy or stream it. Okay by me whatever you do because I still get those residuals.

That's Hollywood thinking too…